Current Research in Egyptology II

January 2001

Edited by

Ashley Cooke
Fiona Simpson

BAR International Series 1380
2005

Published in 2016 by
BAR Publishing, Oxford

BAR International Series 1380

Current Research in Egyptology II

ISBN 978 1 84171 820 0

© The editors and contributors severally and the Publisher 2005

The authors' moral rights under the 1988 UK Copyright,
Designs and Patents Act are hereby expressly asserted.

All rights reserved. No part of this work may be copied, reproduced, stored,
sold, distributed, scanned, saved in any form of digital format or transmitted
in any form digitally, without the written permission of the Publisher.

BAR Publishing is the trading name of British Archaeological Reports (Oxford) Ltd.
British Archaeological Reports was first incorporated in 1974 to publish the BAR
Series, International and British. In 1992 Hadrian Books Ltd became part of the BAR
group. This volume was originally published by Archaeopress in conjunction with
British Archaeological Reports (Oxford) Ltd / Hadrian Books Ltd, the Series principal
publisher, in 2005. This present volume is published by BAR Publishing, 2016.

Printed in England

PUBLISHING

BAR titles are available from:

	BAR Publishing
	122 Banbury Rd, Oxford, OX2 7BP, UK
EMAIL	info@barpublishing.com
PHONE	+44 (0)1865 310431
FAX	+44 (0)1865 316916
	www.barpublishing.com

CONTENTS

FOREWORD ii

SYMPOSIUM PAPERS NOT INCLUDED IN THIS VOLUME iii

THE USE OF THE DOUBLE AND TRIPLE URAEUS IN ROYAL ICONOGRAPHY 1
Sally-Ann Ashton

THE ORGANISATION AND MOBILISATION OF OLD KINGDOM QUARRY LABOUR
FORCES AT CHEPHREN'S QUARRY (GEBEL EL-ASR) LOWER NUBIA. 11
Elizabeth Bloxam

EXCAVATIONS AT THEBAN TOMB KV 39 21
Ian Buckley

AN OLD KINGDOM TOWN AT ZAWIET SULTAN (ZAWIET MEITIN) IN MIDDLE EGYPT:
A PRELIMINARY REPORT 29
Nadine Moeller

EGYPT AND MYCENAEAN GREECE: A MYCENEAN PERSPECTIVE 39
Georgina Muskett

THE AGE OF THE SPHINX AND THE DEVELOPMENT OF THE GIZA NECROPOLIS 47
Colin Reader

THE TRANSITION TO STATE SOCIETY IN EGYPT: PROBLEMS AND POSSIBILITIES OF
APPLYING MORTUARY EVIDENCE 57
Joanne Rowland

SINGLE MOTHER GODDESSES AND DIVINE KINGSHIP: THE SIDELOCK OF YOUTH AND
THE MATERNAL BOND 65
Geoffrey Tassie

MORPHOLOGICAL VARIATIONS IN EGYPTIAN CRANIA 75
Sonia Zakrzewski

FOREWORD

In January 2000 Dr. Angela McDonald and Dr. Christina Riggs of Oxford University started a wonderful thing: Current Research in Egyptology. In the dark days before this there was little or no chance of Egyptology research students from different institutions meeting together in one venue to discuss their current research. The symposium was a great success and is now a regular annual event that has been hosted by a number of other universities: Birmingham, London, Durham and most recently, Cambridge. The success of CRE lies in one of its initial aims, 'to foster communication and the exchange of ideas'. This is achieved not only in the professional forum of a lecture hall, but also, and perhaps more importantly, over a meal and in local hostelries. It is therefore with great regret that it has taken some time for this publication of the Liverpool CRE II to appear in print and we offer our apologies.

On 18-19 January 2001, 34 speakers from ten different institutions came together in Liverpool to present papers on their current research in the field of Egyptology. With many of the symposium members working within the six World Heritage sites of Egypt it seemed only fitting that the venue should be held at the Albert Dock, itself part of the famous Liverpool skyline, that is also deservedly a World Heritage site. The lecture theatre of the Merseyside Maritime Museum amply accommodated the speakers and a full audience that had come to hear a set of fascinating papers. At the close of the first day a meal was held in the agreeable Georgian ambience of Staff House, allowing for more informal chat.

Not all papers presented at the symposium are included in this volume and we have compiled a list of speakers and their paper titles that do not appear here with the collected published papers. Many speakers have published their work as part of a larger study in other places, such as Sami Uljas, whose paper he presented at CRE II was selected as a winner for the Basel Egyptology Student Prize. Like some other CRE publications, abbreviations for periodicals and reference work adhere to the conventions of the *Lexikon der Ägyptologie*, vol. 7, edited by E. Otto and W. Westendorf (Wiesbaden: Harrassowitz, 1992).

A great deal of people assisted with the organisation of the symposium and in many ways they ensured an enjoyable two days. For more than generous sponsorship we are grateful to the Humanities Graduate School of the University of Liverpool and to Prof. Elizabeth Slater, then Head of the School of Archaeology, Classics and Egyptology. Dr. Piotr Bienkowski assisted with the booking of the venue and we are grateful to him for his inside advice that allowed us to host the symposium in such congruous surroundings. Dr. Angela McDonald and Dr. Christina Riggs have provided great advice from their experience of running CRE I in Oxford. Dr. Mark Collier, Prof. Ken Kitchen, Dr. Ian Shaw and Dr. Steven Snape of SACE not only agreed to present papers on their current research but they have also provided valuable support and advice throughout and we would like to thank them. The trooper Pat Winker was unfailing with her help in mailing colleagues, accounts and the organisation of the delightful evening meal held in Staff House. Many friends and colleagues rallied round before, during, and after the symposium and in particular we would like to thank Dr. Debbie Hunter, Dr. Katerina Koltsida, Dr. Sherine El-Menshawy, Dr. Akiko Sugi, Dr. Susanna Thomas and Sami Uljas. In more recent times the exceptional company of Jon Hogg and Glenn Godenho and has made the task of editing this volume slightly less arduous, despite a whole range of difficulties.

CRE has just recently been hosted by Cambridge University, organised by Rachel Mairs and Alice Stevenson. Following an enthusiastic response for papers the symposium was extended to three days, exemplifying the current growth of the subject and the dying need of CRE. It would seem CRE has gone full swing and will next be hosted at Oxford University and we wish the best of luck to the organisers.

Ashley Cooke
Fiona Simpson
December 2004.

Symposium Papers not Included in this Volume

'The religious and social customs of New Kingdom Gurob from the Manchester Collection'
Audrey Carter, The University of Manchester

'Lahun Papyri'
Mark Collier, The University of Liverpool

'Kahun: A glimpse of the Middle Bronze Age'
Ashley Cooke, The University of Liverpool

'Egyptomania'
Rachael Dann, TheUniversity of Durham

'Textual criticism and Ipuwer'
Roland Enmarch, University College, Oxford

'Harbours' and 'quays' in the Nile valley: a novel solution to the problem of the fluctuating river level'
Angus Graham, University College, London

'An ethnoarchaeological investigation of the Festival of Opet'
Hiroshi Hirayama, Wasada University

'Tutankhamun's body armour: materials, construction and the implications for the Late Bronze Age military industry'
Thomas D. Hulit, The University of Durham

'Hatshepsut's femaleness as an ideological force in the Speos Artemidos inscription'
Deborah Hunter, The University of Liverpool

'Far-flung frontiers in Egyptological-related research'
K. A. Kitchen, The University of Liverpool

'Space and gender in Ancient Egyptian village households'
Katerina Koltsida The University of Liverpool

'Cat versus snake: A symbolic conflict with magical connotations'
Panagiotis Kousoulis, The University of Liverpool

'Memphis: questioning the Old Kingdom capital'
Serena Love, University College, London

'The orthography of fear. Bird determinatives in Ancient Egyptian'
Angela McDonald, Worcester College, Oxford

'Petrie and the origin of the underclass'
Bill Manley, National Museums of Scotland, Edinburgh

'Gloves in Ancient Egypt'
Sherine el-Menshawy, The University of Liverpool

'What's in a toponym? On Egyptian and Greek names for Ptolemaic settlements'
Katja Mueller, Peterhouse, Cambridge

'The priests and officials at Thebes during the Twenty-Fifth Dynasty in Egypt'
Chris Naunton, The University of Birmingham

'The emerald mines in the Sikait-Subara region of the Eastern Desert'
Ian Shaw, The University of Liverpool

'The use of stable isotopes to reconstruct Ancient Egyptian diet'
Andrew Shortland, Mike Richards and Sonia Zakrzewski, The Research Laboratory for Archaeology and the History of Art, Oxford

'The Libyan in Egyptian ideology'
Fiona Simpson, The University of Liverpool

'Excavations at Zawiyet Umm el-Rakham'
Steven Snape, The University of Liverpool

'Aspects of Egyptian iconography'
Akiko Sugi, The University of Liverpool

'Ramesses II in the Western Delta'
Susanna Thomas, The University of Liverpool

'The human body in the Pyramid Texts'
Aloisia de Trafford, *University College, London*

'Notions on interclausal relations in Middle Egyptian object complementation with the infinitive'
Sami Uljas, The University of Liverpool

'Can an Egyptian's name shed light on their religious beliefs? References to goddesses in personal names from 1070 to 332 BC'
Nina Wahlberg, The University of Birmingham

THE USE OF THE DOUBLE AND TRIPLE URAEUS IN ROYAL ICONGRAPHY

Sally-Ann Ashton

This paper is intended as a brief survey of the double and triple uraeus from the Eighteenth to the Ptolemaic dynasties with further thoughts on the interpretation and meaning of multiple cobras, as used in Egyptian royal iconography. As a hieroglyph the cobra was used as a determinative for a goddess, but the uraeus was perhaps the most obvious mark of kingship and thus royalty; associated with the sun god Ra and with the goddess Hathor as the eye of Ra, it was believed that it offered protection to kings, and later queens of Egypt, against their enemies. It has also been suggested that the uraeus was linked to female deities and the solar myth, and that it was used to link the queen to Hathor, as the daughter and eye of Ra. The double form of uraeus is a feature which is often noted but rarely explained in catalogues which range from the Eighteenth Dynasty to the Ptolemaic period; its appearance is sporadic, and with the exception of the Twenty-fifth Dynasty Kushite kings, its use is reserved in statuary for royal women. Here, it is important to distinguish between relief and sculptural representations, because the two are rarely consistent. Members of the royal family who wear the double uraeus on statuary are, with the exception of Nefertiti, not usually shown to wear this form on relief representations. Temple relief representations are also an exception in terms of the association of the multiple uraei with male rulers, who often appear with two or more uraei decorating their crowns. There is also a relief representation, or trial piece of Amenhotep III, showing the ruler with a second uraeus at the side of his wig; a motif and form which appeared later on images of Nefertiti.[1]

The earliest example of the use of the double uraeus is in the Eighteenth Dynasty. The principal wife of Ahmose, Nefertari, appears on the relief of the east wall of the tomb of Tetaky, along with titles: 'Daughter of the King, Sister of the King, Wife of the King, Wife of the God, Nefertari, Living Forever'.[2] The double form appears on a basalt statue of Isis, who was the wife of Tutmosis II and the mother of Tutmosis III, from Karnak. On the back pillar the queen takes the title 'mother of the king'; the cobras also wear the crowns of Upper and Lower Egypt, a feature which also occurs on the statues of Queen Tiye and which might suggest that the double form refers to the unification of Upper and Lower Egypt (fig. 1). However, too few images of the Queen Isis survive to know if this was standard practise.[3] Tiye frequently appears with the double form: one cobra wearing the white crown of Lower Egypt and the other the red crown of Upper Egypt, thus representing the joining of the two lands. On the Medinet Habu statue and on another fragment of a statue of Tiye, also now in the Cairo, the queen also wears a vulture headdress; the accompanying head of the vulture separates the two cobras, thus forming another a triad. The vulture wig was a symbol of divine status and this feature is commonly found on temple relief representations and images of goddesses.

Following the accession of Amenhotep IV, the single uraeus was initially used by the royal women, as illustrated by the relief representation of Nefertiti or Tiye, where the queen also wears the crown of Hathor (fig. 2).[4] It is possible that Nefertiti used the single uraeus initially to distinguish between herself and the king's mother, later adopting the double form. The double uraeus only appears on some of the relief representations, and on one colossal sculpture representing Nefertiti from Karnak. The latter has been identified as the queen rather than her husband on account of the double form; her features mimic those of the ruler, with exaggerated features and an elongated face.[5] The uraei of Nefertiti are never adorned with the crowns of Upper and Lower Egypt, they do, however often wear the sun-disk with cows' horns, as seen on the Petrie Museum fragment (fig. 3). The queen did, however, use the title 'Lady of the Two Lands', continuing the tradition of earlier Eighteenth Dynasty queens.[6] There is also the possibility of a second co-regency, which some scholars believe, from epigraphic evidence, occurred during the later years of Akhenaten's rule, regnal year 16 or 17.[7] However, if Aldred's artistic chronology is accepted, the double uraeus appears in the early part of the queen's rule; interestingly on the stelae, the double form appears on group representations that feature other members of the royal family.[8] Meritaten continued the tradition of the double uraeus, as illustrated by a stela showing the princess with her consort; the two cobras are decorated with sun disks and cows' horns, as on some of the images of her mother.[9]

The well-known relief showing Akhenaten and Nefertiti with the three princesses, which was dated to year eight of their reign, now in the Aegyptisches Museum, Berlin

---

[1] Aegyptisches Museum, Berlin inv. 21.299.
[2] De Garis Davies 1925, 14, pl. II.
[3] Porter and Moss 1972, 144; Troy 1986, 164, 18.17.
[4] Green 1997, 9-10.
[5] Arnold in Arnold 1997, 17 quoting Eaton-Krauss 1981, 217, n. 3. Russmann identified the statues with a double uraeus as Akhenaten: 1974, 38 f.n. 1, this seems unlikely given that all of the relief representations with this feature show that it was associated with Nefertiti.
[6] Arnold 1997, 85.
[7] Allen, 1991, 74-85; Murnane 1995, 205-8.
[8] Aldred 1973, 57.
[9] Aldred 1973, 188, no. 120.

Fig. 1. Courtesy of the Egyptian Museum, Cairo (JE 42072). Photograph by the author.

Fig. 2. Copyright Petrie Museum of Egyptian Archaeology (UC 038).

and thought to have originated from Amarna, shows an intriguing development in the iconography of Nefertiti, in that she has three rather than two cobras decorating her crown: one in the centre of her headdress, but with two other cobras at the side of her crown (fig. 4).[10] On the relief, the princess Ankhesenpaaten reaches upwards and holds one of the cobras in her hand. Whether the third is to be seen as an artistic rather than ideological development or deviation cannot be known for certain, but it is not until the end of the Ptolemaic period that the triple uraeus was used with any consistency and in statuary. A sculptors' model from the Aten temple at Amarna, shows an artists attempts to carve the two cobras at the side of the head; the usual central uraeus in this instance has not been added to the relief.[11] This feature also appears on the model relief of Amenhotep III.

The double uraeus appeared again on the representations of the Nineteenth Dynasty queen and daughter of Ramesses II, Meritamun, as seen on the statue of the queen from the Ramesseum at Thebes, and now in the Egyptian Museum, Cairo (fig. 5).[12] On a Third Intermediate Period statue of Shepenwepet I from Medinet Habu, now in the Egyptian Museum Cairo, the double cobras are decorated with cows' horns, and sun disks, linking the queen to Hathor and perhaps representing the eyes of Ra, instead of Upper and Lower

---

[10] Aldred 1973, 102, no. 16.

[11] Cairo, Egyptian Museum JE 592964, Arnold in Arnold 1997, 67, fig. 62.
[12] Borchardt 1925, 152, pl. 108, CG 600 (JE 31413).

Fig. 3. Copyright Petrie Museum of Egyptian Archaeology (UC 401).

Fig. 4. Courtesy of the Aegyptisches Museum, Berlin und Papyrussammlung SMPK. Copyright M. Buesing (14145).

Fig. 5. Reproduced courtesy of the Egyptian Museum, Cairo (CG 600). Photograph Petrie Museum Archives.

Egypt.[13] Once again the cobras decorate the sun disk on the crown rather than the forehead of the statue, as seen on the images of Nefertiti on the sarcophagus of Akhenaten. Amenirdis I, who was chosen as Shepenwepet's successor as God's Wife also has two cobras, but with no regalia; this is perhaps a reflection of some of the examples worn by the male rulers of the Twenty-fifth Dynasty where the uraei are not decorated with crowns. Amenirdas also wears a vulture headdress, which shows her in a divine role, however, too few representations of royal women from this period survive to know if the double uraeus and vulture was standard, and if the cobras were always without the crowns of Upper and Lower Egypt.[14] During this period, the double uraeus appears for the first time on statues of the pharaoh. Although rulers appear with multiple uraei on temple reliefs, particularly in the Late, Ptolemaic and Roman periods, only in the Twenty-fifth Dynasty, do the male rulers appear with the double uraeus on statuary, although on relief representation they can appear with multiple uraei decorating on the crown.[15]

The adoption of the double uraeus by Arsinoe II in the Ptolemaic period seems to have occurred early in her reign. On a colossal statue of the queen now in the Vatican Museum, the queen appears with her consort as the Theoi Adelphoi or sibling gods, wearing the double uraeus. The inscription on the back pillar offers some possibilities for understanding the use of the motif: The Princess Inherent, Daughter of Geb, the first, the Daughter of the Bull *mrhw*, the Great Generosity, the Great Favour, King's Daughter, Sister, Spouse, Woman of Upper and Lower Egypt, Image of Isis, Beloved of Hathor, Mistress of the Two Lands, Arsinoe, who is Brother-Loving, Beloved of Atum, Mistress of the Two Lands.[16] Arsinoe's iconography remained consistent, and even on posthumous representations, which can be dated stylistically to the First Century BC, the queen still appears with a double uraeus.[17] Her statues also share stylistic similarities with those of Shepenwepet and Amenirdas, who were themselves associated, especially the styling of the statues with the left hand across the abdomen, which can be found on several images including a Ptolemaic limestone statue with a double uraeus (fig. 7).[18]

Is there then a single meaning of the double uraeus, or a common usage? Robins suggested that the double uraeus, like the double horns and disk, linked the queen to solar worship.[19] The iconography is not, however, constant as in the case of Queen Tiye, who is rarely, if ever, seen without the double uraeus on statuary, which would again support the idea that Nefertiti used it for a specific event or reason. In both cases the distinctive iconography accords with the queens' elevated status and roles of Tiye and of her successor Nefertiti. This usage is, however, unlikely to have been to aid recognition as perhaps later in the Ptolemaic period because the reliefs and statues of Tiye and Nefertiti are usually inscribed.

Sometimes a clue to the meaning of the double uraeus is offered in the form of the crowns of Upper and Lower Egypt which adorn the cobras' heads, which would suggest that the two cobras represented the two lands; although if this really were the case it is difficult to comprehend why the representations of the king himself, whose very being enabled the unification of Egypt, were not, until the Kushite period, embellished with the two

---

[13] Egyptian Museum, Cairo JE 59870.
[14] Russmann 1974, 39.
[15] Russmann 1974, 38 cites examples of the double uraeus on temple reliefs in connection with the Crown of Justice.
[16] Vatican Museo Gregoriano Egizio 25; see Ashton 2001, 38, 100, no. 35, also for earlier bibliography.
[17] Ashton 2001a, 49, 116-17, no. 66,
[18] Corteggiani in Rausch (ed.) 1998, 171, no. 119, also for earlier bibliography.
[19] Robins 1993, 54.

cobras.[20] On the male rulers of the Twenty-fifth Dynasty, Russmann notes the inclusion of the crowns of Upper and Lower Egypt on some of the Kushite cobras, and suggests that the rulers followed tradition rather than suggesting the unification of Egypt and Kush as an alternative.[21] Indeed the two usual symbols for the two lands are the cobra goddess, Wadjet, and the vulture goddess Nekhbet. This unification is represented literally and symbolically on the gold mask of Tutankhamun in the Egyptian Museum, Cairo, with a cobra and a vulture head, each wearing the appropriate crown. Although images of the god Monthu wore the double uraeus from the Middle Kingdom, the use of the double uraeus in royal iconography was reserved for queens until the Twenty-fifth Dynasty.[22]

The crowns appear on the earliest example of the double uraeus, as illustrated by the statue of Isis (fig. 1). During the reign of Queen Tiye cobras are always decorated with the crowns of Upper and Lower Egypt and the vulture appears. Thus iconographically, the vulture headdress was still used to denote divine status and the double cobras, it would seem, were associated with the two lands; which accords to one of the queen's titles: *nbt t3wy*, Mistress of the Two Lands.[23] Following this initial period, however, the crowns disappear; some queens are still associated with the title *nbt t3wy* and on the Vatican statue of Arsinoe II and on the Pithom Stela, the queen is described as *nbt t3wy*. There are, however, no crowns decorating the cobras on any of the pieces associated with Arsinoe.[24] The same is, however, true of many of the sun disks which decorate Ptolemaic temple gateways during this period and the lack of crowns may simply represent a change in artistic or iconographic practices; the meaning of the cobras which accompany the sun disk on architectural monuments must, however, have represented the unification of the two lands even without the crowns and the same could be true of the later appearance of the double uraeus on representations of queens.

It is also possible that the double uraeus may have been associated with a specific event; in the case of Queen Tiye, the double uraeus may have been associated with Amenhotep III's Heb Sed festival, celebrated after thirty years of his rule. The youthful image of the queen now in the Boston Museum of Fine Arts has been associated with the rejuvenation of the queen on account of her husband's festival. The space for the uraeus on the Boston statue is double that of a single uraeus, and so although the cobras are now missing it is likely that this statue was adorned with the double form of the insignia. However, the well-known wooden head of a queen also

Fig. 6. Reproduced courtesy of the Egyptian Museum, Cairo (CG 565), Karnak. Photograph Petrie Museum Archives.

---

[20] See Troy 1986, 122-26.
[21] Russmann 1974, 40 f.n. 4.
[22] Russmann 1974, 40-43 for the consistent association of the double uraeus with deities and 40 footnote 7 for the association of double uraeus of Monthu with the Twenty-fifth dynasty rulers, which she dismisses.
[23] Troy 1986, 166, 18.34.
[24] Troy 1986, 178-79.

Fig. 7. Courtesy of the Egyptian Museum, Cairo (CG 678). Photograph by author.

originally had a single uraeus, but the wig and headdress were remodelled. It has been noted that the khat headdress, which was part of the original, was worn by Tiye only at Amenhotep III's Heb Sed festival, and was thus adorned with a single uraeus, which must also have been associated with this festival.[25] The image is commonly identified as Tiye, but it has been suggested that it dates from the reign of Akhenaten. The later additions, along with the lack of parallels for the wig might suggest that the piece was re-used for a later queen and that the new identity required a new iconography.[26] In year three of his reign, Akhenaten celebrated his Heb Sed festival; it has been suggested that this festival commemorated his thirtieth birthday rather than the usual thirty year rule. It is possible that the double uraeus was used to stress the role of the queen, who like her predecessor played an important role in the festival. However, Aldred dated the Berlin relief, illustrated in fig. 1, and showing Nefertiti with the double uraeus, to year 8 of the reign, which is later than the Sed festival. Therefore, if Aldred's dating of this particular relief is accepted the double uraeus was used on occasions other than the Heb Sed festival, for Nefertiti at least.

It is possible that the double uraeus distinguished principal wives from the others, and this is something that nearly all of the queens have in common. Consistency, was as noted, found on the images of Tiye and it is possible that the double form was used to indicate Tiye's important political role, which is well documented, or her divine status as the female counterpart to the ruler.[27] The appearance of the double uraeus on the statue of Tiye from the mortuary temple of Amenhotep III at Medinet Habu, would accord with the double uraeus being associated with her role as consort.[28] This theme would be repeated in the immediate reign of Nefertiti and Akhenaten, in the case of Meritamun, daughter and consort of Ramesses II and later under Ptolemy II for his sister and wife Arsinoe II. One thing that the queens with the double uraeus have in common is their prominent roles in religion, politics and representational art, and their status as principal wife.

Meritaten continued the tradition of the double uraeus, as illustrated by a stela showing the princess with her consort fulfilling the same role as her mother. Thus, both she and her mother held principal roles when they appeared with the double form of uraeus. Similarly, Meritamun, like her sisters, was given the title of principal wife, which links with the appearance of the double uraeus on the Eighteenth Dynasty royal images. The queen wears the double uraeus with the crowns of Upper and Lower Egypt, but not the vulture cap that had been worn by Tiye; there were therefore only two figures on her brow and the lack of vulture would suggest that the image was not specifically divine.

Tiye's iconographic link to the goddess Hathor, and her adoption of the goddesses' iconography may also help to explain the constancy of the double form of uraeus in her statuary, which may have been used as a bolster to her elevated status and important role.[29] Nefertiti wears the sun disk and cow's horns on the Petrie Museum relief (fig. 3) and the cobras of Shepenwepet are adorned with the same motif.

The double form of uraeus, may, however, have pointed to a more personal divinity or status of the queens with whom it was associated, as suggested by the vulture headdress, which Tiye wore. The double uraeus and sun disks appear against the larger sun disk of the queen's crown on the Sarcophagus of Akhenaten, where Nefertiti appears as a protective goddess, once again fulfilling a divine role.[30] Here, however, the cobra in the centre of the headdress is a single, which accords with the later iconography of the queen, but perhaps the crown hints at an earlier period or role. Such a use is found later in the

---

[25] Arnold 1997, 33, footnote 83 for bibliography and question of a co-regency which would change this observation.
[26] Aldred 1973, 105; See the discussion by Bryan in Kozloff and Bryan 1992, 209-210 and Freed et al 1999, 215.

[27] Markoe and Capel 1997, 111.
[28] Cairo Egyptian Museum JE 33906.
[29] Kozloff and Bryan 1992, 43.
[30] Arnold 1997, 94-5, fig. 85.

Ptolemaic period, on the statue of Arsinoe II, who wears the vulture cap with the characteristic double uraeus decorating the crown.[31]

The examples from the Third Intermediate Period, may be associated with the earliest use of the double uraeus by a queen. Ahmose-Nefertari was not only principal wife but also 'God's Wife of Amun', a title that also appeared in the Nineteenth Dynasty, and a role that would later be taken by Amenirdis I, who was also associated with the double uraeus and vulture headdress (fig. 6).[32] The god's wives of Amun from the Third Intermediate Period also offer an interesting link to Arsinoe II, wife of Ptolemy II in their titulary. The titles adopted by Shepenwepet and Aminirdis in this role naturally link them to the god Amun, and this is something that occurs in the titles of Arsinoe II, who is described as *S3t Imn*, in addition to *S3t Gb* and *S3t Re*.[33] Like Tiye and Nefertiti these women held principal roles and the double uraeus may have been used to represent this status rather than a specific title or role. It is, however, likely that the use of the double uraeus on Late Period statuary influenced the iconography for Arsinoe II, who also needed to be distinguished from her brother's first wife Arsinoe I. The link to Hathor on the inscription on the back pillar of the Vatican statue may also associate Arsinoe to the solar cult; elsewhere when she is associated with Amun, there is a link to the god's wives and their use of the double uraeus. The double uraeus is also paralleled in the Ptolemaic Greek tradition, where the queen carries a double cornucopia, seen also on the reverse of her coins.[34] Perhaps the most obvious link of duality would be Arsinoe's close relationship to her brother and consort, and her elevated status and posthumous deification, which as noted, she shared with many of her predecessors.

In contrast, the posthumous statues of Arsinoe II must have represented the queen as a goddess in her own right, rather than one of the sibling gods, and so the link with Philadelphos, her brother, is not easily explained or supported by this fact. Furthermore, Arsinoe is the only Ptolemaic queen to be associated with the double uraeus, and only one of two to use the double cornucopia, as illustrated by the coinage and inscribed statuary. The choice of this distinctive iconography for such an early queen must have been deliberate, and perhaps as noted, influenced by the women of the Twenty-Third and Twenty-Fifth dynasties. This inspiration may also have come directly from the re-use of Eighteenth Dynasty material in the Ptolemaic Period, which includes one Amarna-style female from Karnak, in the Second Century BC; it is possible that sculptors looked to earlier periods in order to create the number of statues and images required of this new, foreign dynasty and royal cults.[35] Arsinoe, however, became a role model for perhaps the best well-known Ptolemaic queen- Cleopatra VII and under this particular queen we see a development and addition of a third uraeus for the first time on statuary in the round.[36]

The triple uraeus has caused considerable contention, with some scholars refusing to accept its existence, preferring instead to interpret the triple form as an interpretation of the double uraeus plus a central vulture head.[37] Seven statues have been identified with the triple uraeus, and of these only one shows the queen wearing a vulture cap; this feature appears, however, to have been ignored and the figures are not like those on the statues of earlier queens.[38] On the Leiden statue the two cobras, which identify the subject as Arsinoe II, have been placed on the lower section of her crown; the vulture head sits on the queen's forehead. Unfortunately none of the statues are inscribed and so there is no clue as to the meaning of the triple uraeus. Bothmer suggested, in his identification of a statue with a triple uraeus as Cleopatra II, that the three cobras represented one of the queen's triple rules, with her two brothers Ptolemies VI and VIII or with Ptolemy VIII and Cleopatra III.[39] If, however, as seen in the case of Arsinoe II, the double form was used for both the queen's posthumous representations, any link with another person is implausible because it would cause confusion. This is true of the earlier uses of the double uraeus, where the only possible link with the king would be that the queen was distinguishable on account of the iconography rather than literally representing the royal couple. On some of the purely Egyptian-style images representing Cleopatra VII, the same pose with the hand across the lower abdomen that was found on the images of Arsinoe and Amenirdas, is repeated. This may suggest the copying of statuary and is unusual in the Ptolemaic period because the pose rarely occurs in the two hundred years or so, separating the reigns of the two queens. Possibly the earliest example of the triple uraeus occurs on a crown from Koptos which was originally thought to represent Arsinoe II, but has recently been re-identified as a fragment of an image of Cleopatra VII. The inscription on the back pillar, which is only partially preserved reads: column 1) Hereditary noble, great of praise, mistress of Upper and Lower Egypt, contented... column 2) kings' daughter, king's sister, great royal wife, who satisfies the heart of Horus. Again, the title *nbt t3wy* appears in

---

[31] Arnold 1997, for a discussion of the divine status of Nefertiti and fig. 85 for the sarcophagus fragment, now in the Egyptian Museum, Berlin. For the Leiden representation of Arsinoe II see Ashton 2001a, 100, no. 37.
[32] Borchardt 1925, 114-15, pl. 96, also for inscription of CG 565; Robins 1993, 43, 153-56 see also Marcoe and Capel 1997, 115, no. 48.
[33] Troy 1986, 177 and 178.
[34] Ashton 2000, 1-2.

[35] The re-use of earlier statuary is the subject of a paper by Ashton: 'The Ptolemaic royal image and the Egyptian tradition', in W.J. Tait (ed.) *'Never had the like occurred': Egypt's view of its past. Encounters with Ancient Egypt*, a conference held at the Institute of Archaeology, London, 16th-18th December 2000 (forthcoming University of Pennsylvania Press). For the royal cults and images see Ashton 2001, 16-19.
[36] See Ashton 2001a, 40-42 and 48-49 for identification of this group, and in Walker and Higgs (eds.) 2001, 148-55.
[37] Müller in Bothmer 1960, 147.
[38] Turin, Egyptian Museum see Ashton 2001, 100-01, no. 38.
[39] Bothmer 1960, 145-46, inv. 89.2.660.

connection with, in this instance, the triple uraeus but earlier, as noted with the double form. Various suggestions have been made as to the possible meaning of the triple form of uraeus, although none to date have been terribly satisfactory.

The most recent discussion of the Petrie Museum crown, suggests that it was associated with the bark shrine of Cleopatra, and was dedicated during a period very early in her reign, when she ruled with her second brother Ptolemy XIV. If this association is correct then the previous interpretations of the meaning of three cobras such as territorial or ideological are unlikely.[40]

Cleopatra VII's divinity was apparent from the start of her rule, even during the period of her co-rule with Ptolemy XIII, as illustrated by the Greek inscription on a stela now the Musée du Louvre, Paris where Cleopatra is described as Philopator (father-loving) and thea (goddess); thus referring to her place within the dynastic and to her personal cult.[41] Like the images of Arsinoe II, the triple uraeus appears on both the purely Egyptian-style images representing the queen in a more general role as ruler or as part of the dynastic cult, and on the Egyptian-style images with Greek attributes such as a cornucopia or cork-screw wig. This would imply that the triple form was associated with more than one role of the queen, unlike the images of Nefertiti for instance, when the double uraeus only appears on a specific occasion, often in this particular queen's case when she appears with her family, as seen on fig. 3.

The double uraeus initially seems to be associated with the elevation of a queen either to principal wife or mother of the king, this may have been to distinguish a particular royal female from others, such as other wives or in the case of Tiye and Nefertiti, the current wife of the king, respectively. Even when the inscriptional evidence is considered, there seems to be no one aspect or title in common between the various periods, nor are the queens consistent in their use of the double uraeus. Tiye, and Arsinoe II adopt the motif consistently, whereas with other queens either too few statues survive to know if it was part of their standard iconography, or in the case of Nefertiti, the double form only appears on certain occasions. Then, there is Cleopatra VII with the triple form of the uraeus, a motif that associates her with Arsinoe II, but also distinguishes her from her role model and any previous queens. Such a development, in what was to be the final years of Ptolemaic rule is perhaps only to be expected of this particular queen. The identification of this group of statuary and our understanding of Cleopatra's image are only just beginning to be appreciated. It is possible perhaps that the multiple uraeus could represent different ideas or ideologies throughout the history of Egyptian royal representation and that above all else it marked its wearers above the other women who surrounded them, and in the case of Cleopatra VII, the men who surrounded her.

Acknowledgements

The author would like to thank: Dr Stephen Quirke for his helpful comments on the original text, Dr Roberta Shaw for her comments and bibliographic references. Dr Christian Loeben for his help with obtaining an image of figure 4. The Aegyptisches Museum, Berlin and the Egyptian Museum, Cairo for permission to reproduce images of their objects.

Sally-Ann Ashton
Fitzwilliam Museum
Cambridge

Cited works

Aldred, C.
   1973 *Akhenaten and Nefertiti* New York: The Brooklyn Museum.

Allen, J.
   1991 'Akhenaten's 'Mystery' co-regent and successor', *Amarna Letters* Essays *on Ancient Egypt, c. 1390-1310 BC* 1: 74-85. San Francisco: Sebastopol CAKMY Communications.

Arnold, D. (ed.)
   1997 *The Royal Women of Amarna. Images of Beauty from Ancient Egypt.* New York: The Metropolitan Museum of Art.

Ashton, S-A.
   2000 'The Ptolemaic influence on Egyptian royal sculpture', in A. McDonald and C. Riggs (eds.) *Current Research in Egyptology 2000.* BAR International Series 909. Oxford: BAR Publishing.
   2001a *Ptolemaic Royal Sculpture From Egypt.* BAR International Series 923. Oxford: BAR Publishing.
   2001b 'Identifying the Egyptian-style Ptolemaic Queens', in S. Walker and P. Higgs (eds.) *Cleopatra of Egypt: from History to Myth.* London: British Museum Press: 148-55.

Borchardt, L.
   1925 *Statuen und Statuetten von Koenigen und Privatleuten.* Catalogue Général des Antiquités Égyptiennes du Musée du Caire 2. Berlin: Reichsdruckerei.

De Garis Davies, N.
   1925 'The tomb of Tetaky at Thebes (no. 15)' *JEA* 11: 10-18.

---

[40] Petrie Museum of Egyptian Archaeology UC 14521; see Ashton 2001a, 67 and 'Cleopatra and the Egyptian tradition', Margaret M. Miles (ed.) (forthcoming University of California Press). Ashton 2001b, 154-55 for the meanings of the triple uraeus.
[41] Étienne in Walker and Higgs (eds.) 2001, 156-57, no. 154.

Eaton-Kraus, M.
  1981 'Miscellanea Amarnesia', *Chronique D'Égypte* 56: 245-64.
Green, L.
  1997 'The royal women of Amarna: who was who?', in D. Arnold (ed.) *The Royal Women of Amarna. Images of Beauty from Ancient Egypt.* New York: The Metropolitan Museum of Art: 7-16.
Kozloff, A.P. and B.M. Bryan
  1992 *Egypt's Dazzling Sun.* Cleveland: The Cleveland Museum of Art.
Murnane, W.J
  1995 *Texts from the Amarna Period in Egypt.* Atlanta: Scholars Press.
Markoe, G.E. and K. Capel.
  1996 *Mistress of the House, Mistress of Heaven : women in ancient Egypt.* New York: Hudson Hills Press.

Porter, B. and L.B. Moss.
  1972 *Topographical bibliography of ancient Egyptian hieroglyphic texts, reliefs and paintings 2, Theban temples* - 2nd ed. Oxford: Griffith Institute.
Rausch, M. (ed.)
  1989 *La Gloire d'Alexandrie.* Paris: AFAA.
Robins, G.
  1993 *Women in Ancient Egypt.* London: British Museum Press.
Russmann, E.R.
  1974 *The Representation of the King in the XXVth Dynasty.* Monographies Reine Élisabeth 3. Brooklyn: The Brooklyn Museum.
Troy, L.
  1986 *Patterns of Queenship in ancient Egyptian myth and history.* Uppsala Studies in Ancient Mediterranean and Near Eastern Civilisations 14. Uppsala: Boreas.

THE ORGANISATION AND MOBILISATION OF OLD KINGDOM QUARRY LABOUR FORCES AT CHEPHREN'S QUARRY (GEBEL EL-ASR) LOWER NUBIA

Elizabeth Bloxam

Introduction

Chephren's Quarry, located in the Western Desert of Lower Nubia at Gebel el-Asr (Fig. l), defines an area of quarry workings that cover an area of approximately 120 km² south of Wadi Tushka and 65 km northwest of Abu Simbel. The northern fringe of the quarry is close to the newly excavated Sadat Canal and the Wadi Tushka (Fig. 2). Exploitation of Chephren's Quarry dates from the late Predynastic Period (c.3500 BC) to the Old and Middle Kingdoms (c.2649-1640 BC) and presents an almost pristine, relatively undisturbed archaeological site due to the dry environment and isolation from the Nile floodplain.

Chephren's Quarry is the only known source in Egypt of the uniquely characteristic blue gneisses (hard stone), termed gabbro-gneiss (blue-banded) and anorthosite gneiss (blue speckled). The use of this stone is only known in royal or elite contexts, such as the Fourth Dynasty seated statue of Khafra, which is made from the gabbro-gneiss. The anorthosite gneiss was used, particularly in the Early Dynastic Period (c.2770-2574), for small stone vessels, large quantities of which were found in the Second Dynasty tomb of Khasekhemwy at Abydos (pl. 1).

This paper presents a theory into how labour forces might have been mobilised to work at remote quarry sites such as Chephren's Quarry, but looks at this question beyond the realm of this being purely via state coercion. The sources of evidence around which this theory is modelled come from fresh Old Kingdom settlement evidence excavated at Chephren's Quarry in April 2000, comparative data from other Old Kingdom quarries, texts and the use of anorthosite gneiss during the Early Dynastic Period. The interpretation of this data uses a social theoretical model with which to explore the use of alcohol as a coercive mechanism to mobilise quarry labour forces.

Survey and excavations of a bakery at Khufu Stele Quarry Settlement, Chephren's Quarry

In April 2000 a third season of survey and excavation was undertaken at Chephren's Quarry, directed by Dr. Ian Shaw. In the southern environs of the quarry where only evidence of Old Kingdom quarrying is found, a previously unknown area of settlement exposed as single level dry-stone walled features was located. A modern tarmac road has dissected the settlement and the spoil heaps from this work contain numerous pottery sherds and intact bread moulds (pl. 2). The extent of scattered remains of stone walled features suggests that the original settlement (now called Khufu Stele Quarry Settlement) covered an area of approximately 500 m². On the north side of the tarmac road a small area of the settlement remains relatively undisturbed and comprises three dry-stone walled features. A trial excavation of part of the largest feature (9 m x 7 m) revealed under a deep layer of ash several pits, one containing an intact bread mould (pl. 3). This feature clearly functioned as a bakery and represented the first evidence of in-situ food preparation at Chephren's Quarry. The typology of the bread-moulds dates them to the Early Dynastic Period (First - Third Dynasty) with a possible provenance at Hierakonpolis, Upper Egypt.[1]

This evidence raised three important questions:

1. Does the evidence suggest more permanence to the operation in the Early Dynastic Period?

2. Was the labour force based and thus mobilised from Hierakonpolis?

3. Baking and brewing are usually found together as dual production areas; does this mean that brewing also took place at the quarry?

To approach these questions within the broader issue of how labour might have been mobilised, a social theoretical conceptual framework as outlined below will be applied to the evidence. The aim is to produce a new theory into the mechanisms of labour mobilisation in relation to stone quarrying.

The use of alcohol as a coercive mechanism to mobilise labour

The theme of a "labour-for-beer labour market" in the context of Kushite society in Upper Nubia in the First Millennium BC has been approached as a possible mechanism for labour mobilisation.[2] This concept could be applied to labour mobilisation in the Third Millennium BC and might explain why large quantities of beer jars found at the Hatnub travertine quarry, make up the majority of the pottery corpus there.[3] Pottery recently analysed from the author's recent survey of the Umm es-Sawan gypsum quarry and Widan el-Faras basalt quarry in the Northern Faiyum Desert Lower Egypt, similarly revealed high percentages of containers for alcohol, such as beer and wine jars.

---

[1] Jacquet-Gordon 1981, 12-13.
[2] Edwards 1996, 69.
[3] Shaw (forthcoming)

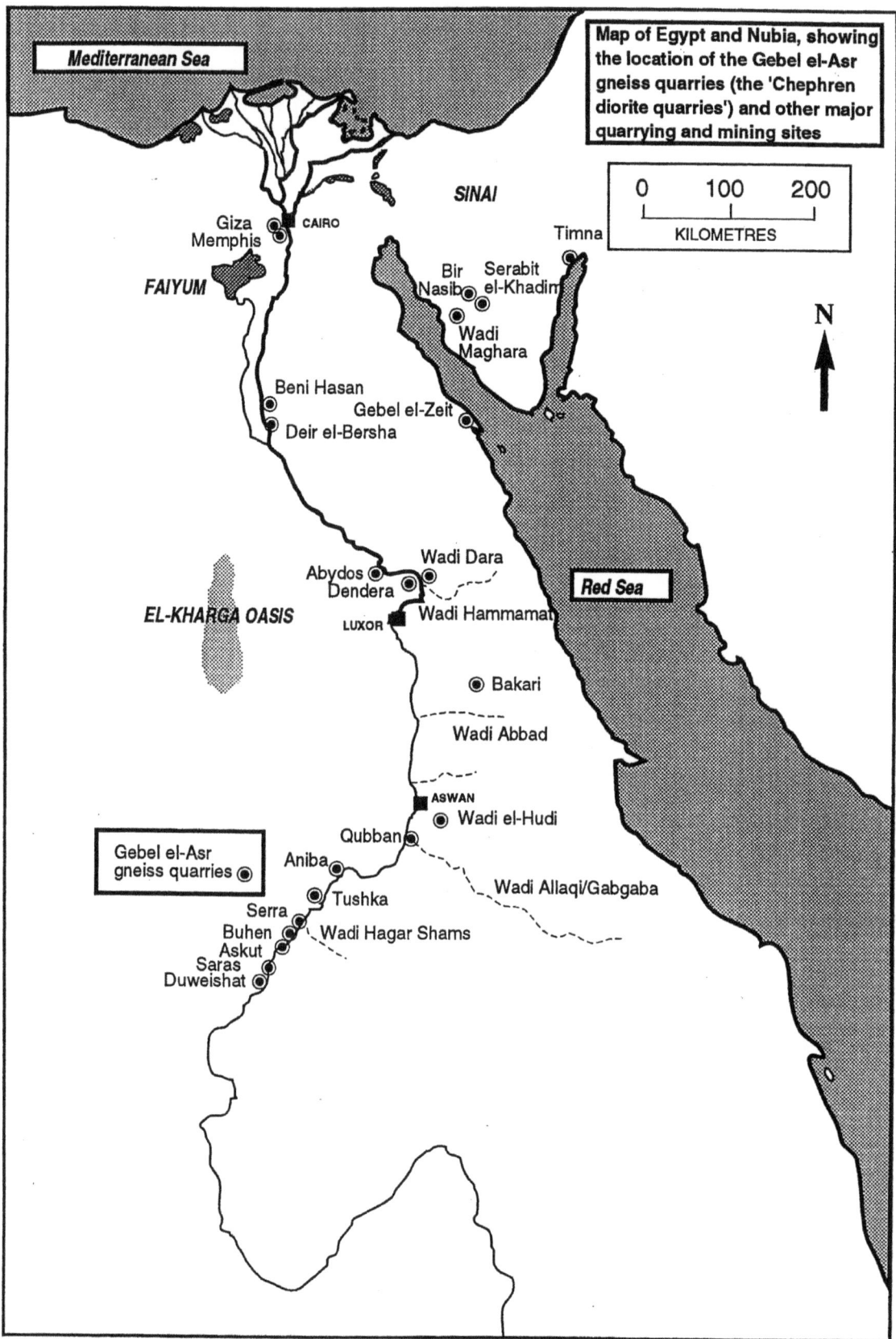

Fig. 1. Pharaonic quarrying and mining sites in Egypt and Nubia. Courtesy of Ian Shaw.

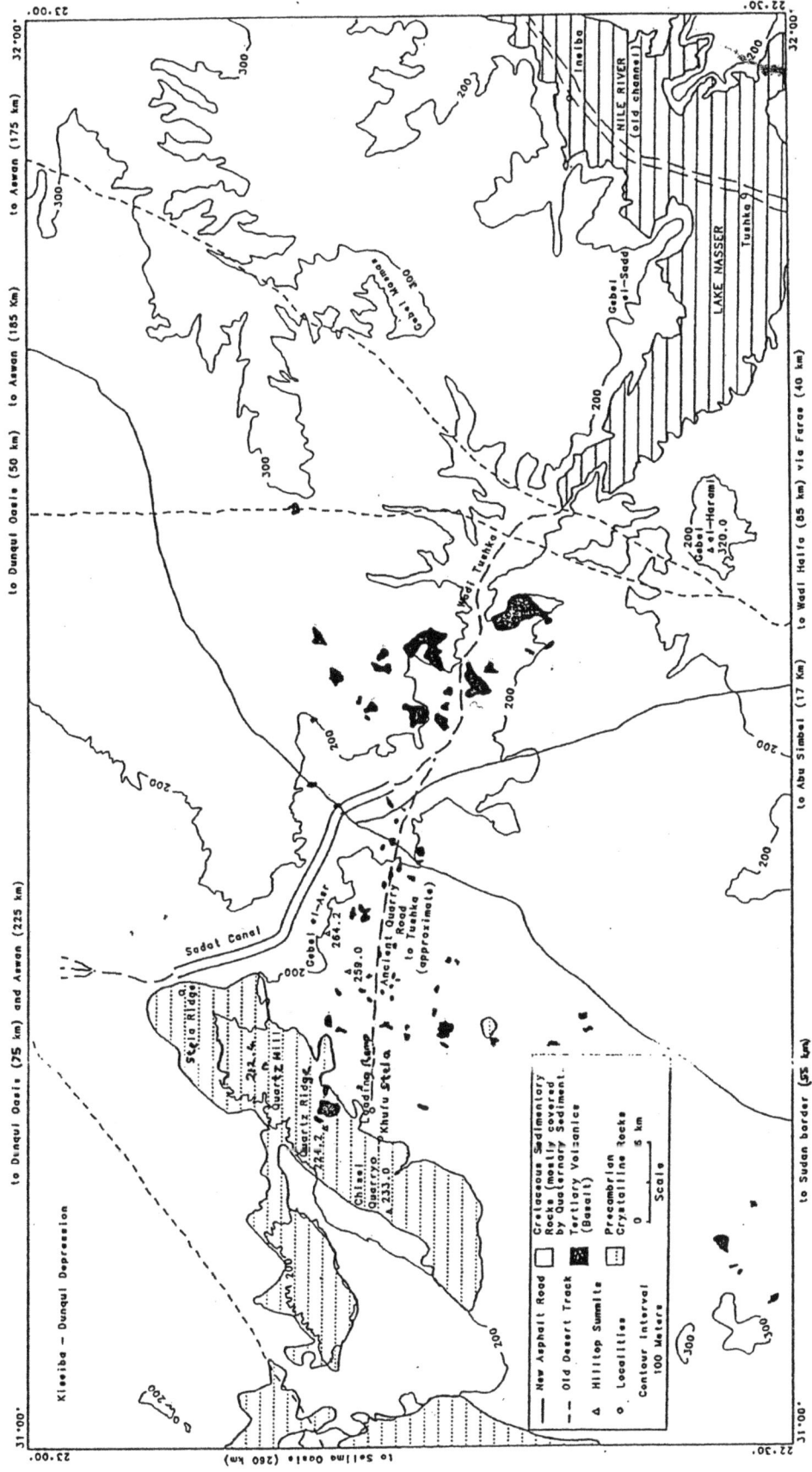

Fig. 2. Topographical and geological map of Chephren's Quarry and the area east to the Nile. After Harrell and Brown 1994: 44.

Pl. 1. Anorthosite gneiss bowl. Early Dynastic Period. Cairo Museum. Author's photograph.

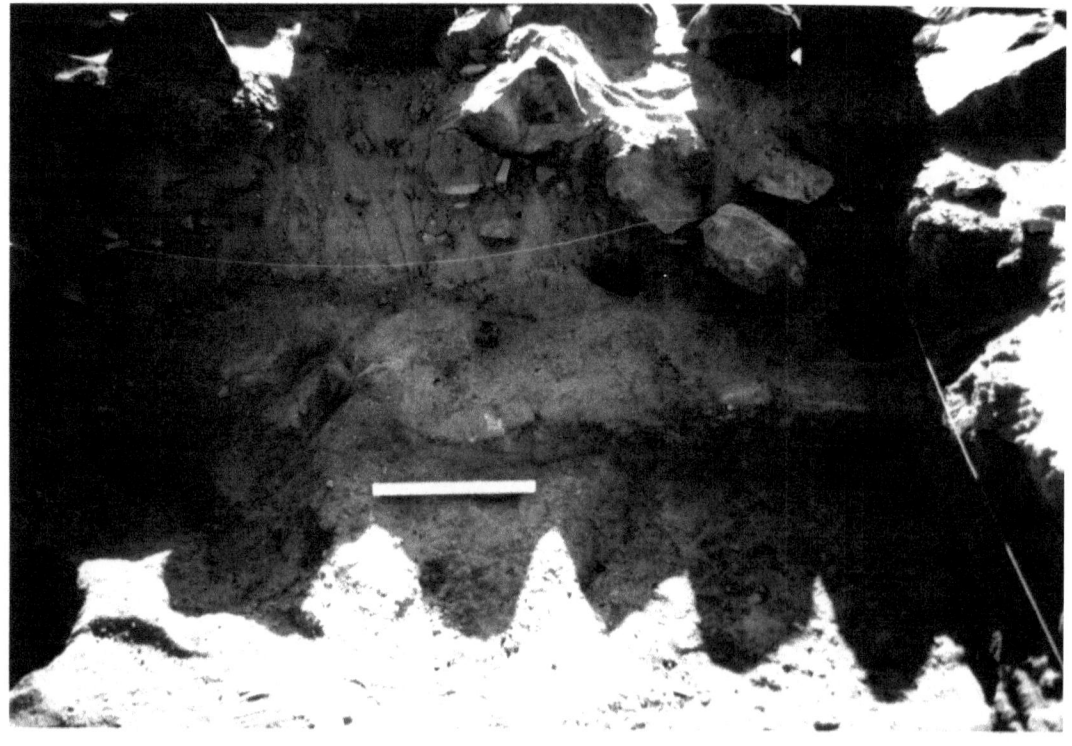

Pl. 2. Bakery at Khufu Stele Quarry Settlement. Author's photograph.

Pl. 3. Bread mould from bakery at Khufu Stele Quarry Settlement. Photograph by Angus Graham.

Using alcohol as a coercive mechanism to mobilise a quarry labour force has hitherto not been connected to this type of evidence. Beer has been mentioned as a method of payment to workers in the Old Kingdom, but not furthered into the social value of alcohol and its use through mechanisms of power to manipulate and mobilise labour forces in complex societies.[4]

The role of alcohol in societies can provide a valuable insight into social systems, so it is surprising how little serious attention this commodity has received until recently, in both anthropological and archaeological research.[5] This is particularly apparent in Egyptian archaeology, which is quite remarkable given that evidence for the production of beer goes back to the Predynastic Period.[6] Large production areas for beer have been found at the Predynastic settlements (early Naqada II) of Hierkonpolis and Abydos.[7] It is also interesting to note that the hieroglyphs for bread and beer are combined to form the generic determinative of 'food'.[8]

A probable reason for alcohol and drinking receiving little attention in explaining aspects of a social system, especially in relation to work, might be due to the negative connotations which are associated with drinking in Western industrialised nations. It is therefore important to contextualise alcohol in pre-industrialised economies where it is consumed in well-defined and controlled social occasions and disassociate it from alcoholism and 'private use'.[9] It thus has to be viewed as a social form that can have, "profound influence in producing changes in social relations and can be informative about society and culture in general".[10]

What archaeological evidence is there for beer being a possible mechanism for mobilising quarry labour forces in a complex society such as Old Kingdom Egypt? As already mentioned, the quarry site of Hatnub reveals a high percentage of beer jars and bread moulds in the corpus of pottery.[11] At Chephren's Quarry evidence for beer consumption had only come from Murray, in a passing reference to finding Middle Kingdom beer jars at a camp close to Quartz Ridge.[12] However, the discovery of an Old Kingdom bakery at Chephren's Quarry has provided fresh evidence to investigate this idea farther, because research to date in Egyptian archaeology places bakeries and breweries in close proximity. The reason for this is because some of the ingredients that go into beer making come from the partial baking of loaves.[13]

With the presence of a bakery at Chephren's Quarry, it can be argued that beer might also have been produced

---

[4] Eyre 1987, 25.
[5] Dietler 1990, 352.
[6] Samuel 2000, 541.
[7] Geller 1989, 51.
[8] Darby, *et al* 1977, 389.

[9] Sherratt 1997, 389.
[10] Dietler 1990, 352.
[11] Shaw (forthcoming)
[12] Murray 1967.
[13] Geller 1992, 19.

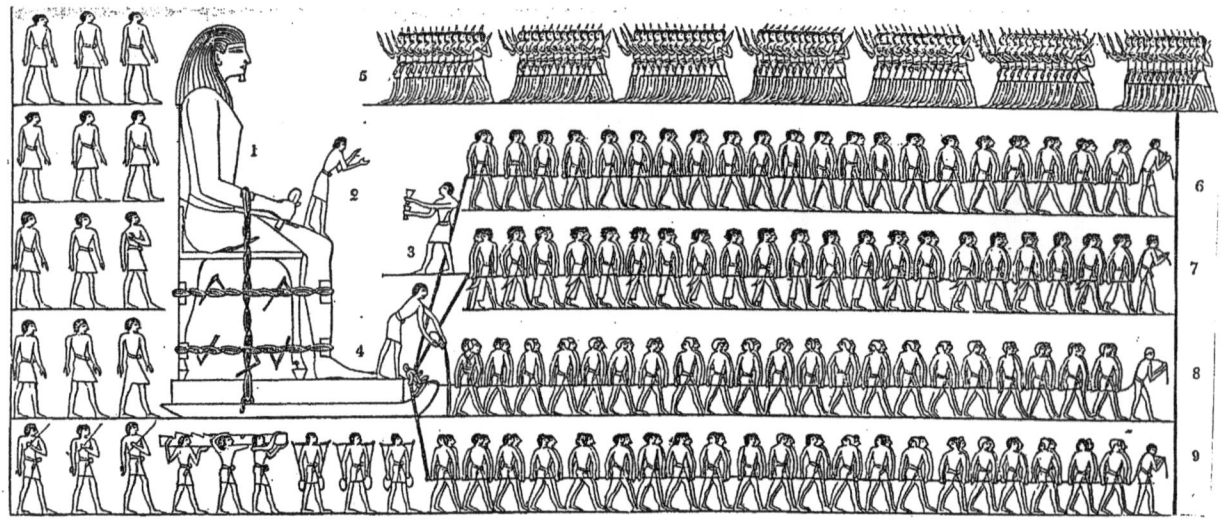

Fig. 3. Transportation scene of Djehutihotpe – Eleventh Dynasty. After Wilkinson 1878, vol. 2:305

in-situ. Evidence to support this idea comes from iconography in which the majority of scenes depicting bread baking also include brewing and could thus be interpreted as dual production activities. This is further supplemented from the archaeological record on the Giza plateau, where excavation of the Fourth Dynasty workmen's settlement provides the evidence which links bread baking and brewing to the same production house.[14] In a religious context bread and beer are also associated as offerings to the gods. A tomb inscription dating to the reign of Sahure (Fifth Dynasty) expresses this, 'to Nekbet, 800 daily offerings of bread and beer; to Buto, 4800 daily offerings of bread and beer; to Re, 138 daily ofierings of bread and beer'.[15] Beer, therefore, performs a variety of functions and roles in society from basic subsistence to ritual offerings to the gods. But despite its ubiquitous nature, the power over production of this commodity was probably not available to all. The control of the production of alcohol is thus crucial in the argument for beer being used as a mechanism to mobilise labour; 'The preparation of alcoholic drinks required investment and ability to concentrate surplus for conspicuous consumption...Such privileges were only available to a few'.[16]

Egypt's economy was based on agricultural subsistence, and, in agriculturally based pre-monetary societies 'feast- driven' mechanisms of labour mobilisation are common in both the historical and ethnographic record.[17] In Mesopotamia, ration-based forms of payment are well documented and clearly connected with central government. Beer belonged to the 'extraordinary rations' that were issued to officials, employees and conscripts of the crown. The Ur 'messenger texts' record the beer rations being distributed to those people, "coming from or going to a certain place, or going for a specific purpose"; this implies that employment on these occasions was only temporary.[18] Thus in the context of Chephren's Quarry one could hypothesise that the mobilisation of a labour force for a specific purpose, could have a similar mechanism of payment and inducement attached to it.

The question as to whether support for a political system was voluntary as well as coerced has been raised,[19] but generally in Egyptian archaeology the idea that, "The mass of people needed for basic labour on any project can only have been provided by corvée, compulsory conscription or national service", is universally believed.[20] But there is only indirect evidence to support this claim.[21] This vision of a robotic coerced labour mass has in essence come from interpreting iconographic depictions, such as the Djehutihotpe colossus literally (fig. 3). The concept of expending large amounts of labour for non-utilitarian purposes would be an integral part of the ideology behind kingship. This outward portrayal might reinforce the king's power base, but was this the reality behind the mobilisation of labour forces? And how could a forced or compulsorily conscripted labour force be maintained?

Even in societies where recourse to coercive power does exist, the mobilisation of labour through work-party feasts and alcohol was employed. In an agricultural-based economic system such as Egypt, it could therefore be suggested that this mechanism was socially embedded.[22] These assertions could be equally applicable to the Old Kingdom, whereby the need to mobilise large labour forces for monumental construction meant that the

---

[14] Lehner 1992.
[15] Darby et al 1977, 503.
[16] Sherratt 1997, 391.
[17] Dietler 1990, 366.
[18] Neumann 1994, 330.
[19] O'Conner 1974, 16.
[20] Eyre 1987, 18.
[21] Eyre 1987, 18.
[22] Dietler 1990, 365, 368-369.

economic role of beer became even more essential part of a complex network of economic relations.

Not only can beer be used to mobilise labour in a complex society, but it might be, "tactically employed as a dynamic element in its formation and maintenance".[23] So, here is presented a commodity, socially embedded, which can mobilise labour forces and maintain power structures. How is this possible? Beer or alcohol has to acquire an economic value through the social context in which it is consumed. Perhaps a tenuous modern analogy would be to that of champagne, which has more elite and social value (in Western society) than any other form of alcoholic beverage, regardless of its monetary value, and thus an essential commodity consumed at important social events. This is called 'commodity by destination'; being an object produced for exchange in the form of consumption within specific social contexts.[24]

Access to surpluses and the control of beer production is therefore crucial and it can be seen that by the latter stages of the Old Kingdom, high officials also had access to beer in exchange for labour. The following text from the tomb of official *Rmnw-kS/Jmj* implies this by saying "I made this tomb in exchange for bread and beer which I gave to the artisans who made this tomb".[25] Similar to the Mesopotamian system, the state or an elite class in a complex society could thus mobilise labour for its own purposes and at the same time maintain inequality via access to this commodity.

Conclusion

How can the social theories outlined above be applied to the archaeological evidence at Chephren's Quarry to argue for beer being used as an inducement to mobilise labour? The presence of a bakery at the site has provided the first evidence of food production occurring here in the Early Dynastic Period (First - Third Dynasty). The bread mould typology dates it between the First and Third Dynasties to Hierakonpolis in Upper Egypt, which coincides with the peak of stone vessel production from anorthosite gneiss in this period.[26] This might imply that the operation could have been organised, on a more permanent basis, from Hierakonpolis. Coincidentally, large production areas of bread making and brewing, dating from Naqada II have been excavated at Hierakonpolis.[27] The size of these installations suggests that there was capacity to produce beer as a surplus, which suggests, "directed production and redistribution by individuals or institutions, chiefdom or temple".[28]

Gender roles also come into play because beer production was generally the domain of women.[29] There are several titles in Egyptian texts that closely associate women with the brewing process, such as 'Controller of the Brewing Women'.[30] This might therefore provide the first indication of women making up a proportion of the quarry labour force.

The evidence discussed above does strongly suggest that beer could have played a pivotal role in the economics of mobilising labour to acquire elite status raw materials. The control of the production of beer, as pointed out earlier, was attached to a state or centrally controlled brewery. It could be farther argued that the beer produced in these breweries was of a higher quality (or had a higher alcohol content) than beer produced at a local level.[31]

How does the use of beer work in the theory of power strategies to mobilise labour for non-utilitarian purposes? The control over production and who has that control is heavily embedded in Marxist materialist thought, in the maintenance of power relations through the relations of production. This might be a too sunplistic way of looking at this aspect and perhaps a more relevant model is Giddens' idea of the "dialectic of labour control",[32] which suggests that agents or individuals either contribute or not to demands made upon them.[33] The idea of 'relational' power, or the capacity to secure an outcome via the actions of others can be well founded in the control of production of beer and its use as a redistributive commodity to exert permanent control over a labour force. The emergence of differential access to a resource is one factor which enables labour to be recruited and mobilised outside of kinship ties and can thus be one of the manifestations of a centralized power base.[34] So perhaps what happened in the fledgling Egyptian state was the manipulative use of a culturally embedded commodity, such as beer, being used as an almost invisible form of coercion by a centralised elite.

In Marxist theory workers would be unconscious of how they were being manipulated due to the over-riding power of state ideology. This powerful state ideology is nowhere more apparent than in ancient Egyptian iconography that represents the world in a limited and artificial way. The power of ideology makes the interests of the few seem like those of the many.[35] The continued control and maintenance of this was the key, demonstrated not only in the volume (in excess of 100,000 m³) of stone transported over distances exceeding 500 miles in the Old Kingdom;[36] but as aptly

---

[23] Sherratt 1995, 14-15.
[24] Appadurai 1986, 4.
[25] Kanawati 1977, 1.
[26] Reisner 1931.
[27] Geller 1989; 1992.
[28] Stol 1994, 179.

[29] Stol 1994, 179.
[30] Darby *et al* 1977, 531.
[31] Snape (*pers comm.* 2001)
[32] Arnold 200, 16.
[33] Giddens 1979.
[34] Arnold 2000, 27.
[35] Giddens 1979.
[36] Röder 1965.

Elizabeth Bloxam

remarked, "The Fourth Dynasty pyramids are an aberration which was never returned to".[37]

Acknowledgments

The author's work at Chephren's Quarry was funded by the Institute of Archaeology, UCL, and doctoral research has been funded by the A.H.R.B. I would like to acknowledge the hard work and support of all the 2000 excavation team members, in particular Richard Lee, Dr. Judith Bunbury, Angus Graham and Debbie Darnell. Special thanks to Dr. Ian Shaw, Director of the Gebel el-Asr project, who made all this possible in the first place. Thanks also to Colin Rogers, Director of El Alsson School in Cairo, for providing us with essential equipment, supplies and storage facilities at the school.

Elizabeth Bloxam
University College London

Cited Works

Appadurai, A.
    1986 'Introduction: commodities and the politics of value', in A. Appadurai(ed.), *The Social Life of Things: Commodities in Cultural Perspectives* Cambridge: Cambridge Univ Press: 3-63.

Arnold, J.E.
    2000 'Revisiting Power, Labor Rights, and Kinship: Archaeology and Social Theory', in M.B. Schifier (ed.) *Social Theory in Archaeology.* Utah: University of Utah Press: 14-30.

Darby, W.J., P. Ghalioungui and L. Grivett
    1977 *Food: The Gift of Osiris.* Vol.2 London: Academic Press

Dietler, M.
    1990 'Driven by drink: the role of drinking in the political economy and the case of early Iron Age France', *JAA* 9:352-406.

Edwards, D.N.
    1996 'Sorghum, beer and Kushite society', *NAR* 29 No.2: 65-77

Eyre, C.J.
    1987 'Work and the Organisation of Work in the Old Kingdom' in M. A. Powell (ed.) *Labor in the Ancient Near East.* Connecticut: American Oriental Society:5-47.

Giddens, A.
    1979 *Central Problems in Social Theory.* London: MacMillan

Geller, J.R.
    1989 'Recent excavation at Hierakonpolis and their relevance to Predynastic production and settlement', *CUPEL* 11: 41-52.

Geller, J.R.
    1992 'Recent Prehistory to history: beer in Egypt', in R. Friedman and B. Adams (eds.), *The Followers of Horus: Studies dedicated to Michael Allen Hoffman 1944-1990.* Exeter: The Short Run Press: 19-26.

Harrell, J.A. and V.M. Brown
    1994 'Chephrm's Quarry in the Nubian Desert of Egypt', *Nubica* 3:43-57

Jacquet-Gordon, H.
    1981 'A tentative typology of Egyptian bread moulds', in D. Arnold (ed.) *Studien zur altägyptischen Kerarmik.* Mainz am Rhein: Verlag Philipp von Zabern:10-15.

Kanawati, N.
    1977 *The Egyptian Administration in the Old Kingdom: Evidence on its Economic Decline.* Warminster: Aris & Phillips.

Lehner.M.
    2000 *Excavations at Giza 1988-1991 The location and Importance of the Pyramid Settlement,* http://www.oi.uchicago.edu/oi/proj/giz/nn_fall 92.html [5/5/00].

Murray, G.W.
    1967 *Dare Me to the Desert.* London: George Allen & Unwin Ltd.

Neumann H
    1994 'Beer as a means of compensation for work in Mesopotamia during the Ur III period', in L. Milano (ed.) *Drinking in Ancient Societies: History and Culture of Drink in the Ancient Near East. Papers of a Symposium held in Rome, May 17-19 1990.* Padova: Sargon srl: 321-331.

O'Connor, D.
    1974 'Poltical systems and archaeological data in Egypt: 2600-1780 B.C.' *World Archaeology* 6:15-38.

Reisner, G.A.
    1931 *Mycerinus: the temples of the third pyramid at Giza.* Cambridge Mass: Harvard University Press.

Roder, J.
    1965 'Zur stembruchgeschichte des rosengranits von Assuan', *AA* 3:467-552

Samuel, D.
    2000 'Brewing and Baking', in P. Nicholson and I.M.E. Shaw (eds.) *Ancient Egyptian Materials and Technology.* Cambridge: Cambridge University Press: 537-576.

Shaw, I.M.E.
    (Forthcoming) 'Site P (The Old Kingdom quarry) and the surrounding settlement', in I.M.E. Shaw (ed.) *The Hatnub Survey.* London: Egypt Exploration Society.

Sherratt, A.
    1995 'Alcohol and its alternatives: symbol and substance in pre-industrial cultures', in J. Goodman, P.E. Lovejoy and A. Sherratt (eds.) *Consuming Habits: Drugs in History and Anthropology.* London, New York: Routledge: 11-46.

---

[37] O'Conner 1974, 17.

Sherratt, A.
　1997　*Economy and Society in Prehistoric Europe: Changing Perspectives.* Edinburgh: Edinburgh University Press.

Stol, M.
　1994　'Beer in Neo-Babylonian Times', in L. Milano (ed.) *Drinking in Ancient Societies: History and Culture of Drinks in the Ancient Near East. Papers of a Symposium held in Rome, May 17-19 1990.* Padova: Sargon srl: 155-183.

Wilkinson, J.G.
　1878　*Manners and Customs of the Ancient Egyptians,* vol.2. London: J. Murray.

EXCAVATIONS AT THEBAN TOMB KV39

Ian Buckley

Introduction

This paper charts some of the experiences of the excavation, work on the tomb, details of the finds and results of the quest to establish the name and title of the tomb owner of KV 39.[1] This tomb was initially published by John Rose, but further research into selected items of evidence by myself, (a principal team member for three seasons and the current Field Director), allows a new interpretation of the evidence to be presented. Importantly, the proposed work to be undertaken this coming season with support from the University of Liverpool is also outlined.

Background and location of the tomb

Theban tomb KV 39 was discovered c.1900, probably by Macarios and Andraos;[2] Weigall and Smith subsequently entered the tomb circa 1908.[3] Weigall described what they found as being entirely ruinous.[4]

The tomb itself lies at the head of the small wadi that runs from the foot of the east face of the mountain peak Meretseger and terminates at a watershed discharging into the gulley, which hides the entrance to the tomb of Tuthmosis III at the southern end of Wadi Biban el-Muluk - the Valley of the Kings. The Valley was used as a royal burial site for over five hundred years and is consequently one of the most excavated areas in Thebes.

Weigall,[5] and more recently Rose,[6] concluded that KV 39's position could very well coincide with the site of the tomb of Amenophis I as described in detail in Papyrus Abbott and translated by Peet from the hieratic text:

"The eternal horizon of King Djeserkara, Sun of Ra, Amenhotep, which measures 120 cubits in depth from its stela (?) called Pa'aka, north of the house of Amenhotep of the Garden".[7]

This hieratic text is a report of an XXth Dynasty inspection of royal tombs and is the primary textual evidence for locating the position of the tomb of Amenophis I. It is a record of the route of the commission sent from Memphis by Ramesses IX in year 16 to inspect a series of tombs suspected of being robbed by the tomb builders from the nearby village of Deir el-Medina. The mountain path leading from the workmen's village of Deir el-Medina to the Valley passes along the ridge by the group of 'workmen's huts', known as the 'way station'. The fact that KV 39 is only 120 cubits (63 metres) down from the stela (?) (called Pa' aka) – interpreted from Papyrus Abbott by Weigall and Rose as being the 'workmen's huts' on the ridge above the tomb, supports this theory. The site of tomb KV 39 below the way station seems to be an ideal spot for the beginning of development for the Valley of the Kings. The depth of 120 cubits is taken as not referring to the actual tomb itself but to the location of the tomb's entrance. Pertaining to the other relevant part of the text in Papyrus Abbott, " north of the house of Amenhotep of the Garden", Rose identified this building with the temple of Amenophis I in the area of the Ptolemaic Temple at Deir el-Medina. This is the nearest monument to the tomb on the ancient Inspectorate's route from the starting point – the administrative centre at Medinet Habu. There is no evidence of a garden here, but KV 39 does lie almost due north of the Temple.[8]

The difficulties of this extract hinge on the exact translation, crucial in identifying accurately the location of the tomb and as Reeves points out, "neither of these landmarks has yet been identified with any certainty on the ground".[9] Nevertheless, situated as it is beneath the natural pyramid shape of Meretseger, by building this early New Kingdom rock cut tomb into the Valley of the Kings there is a suggestion that the tomb builders were adapting the principles of protocol. The cemetery in the Kings' Valley lies at the head of a long wadi, the tombs entrances' being low in the deep valley floor surrounded by the high cliffs of the wadi sides and the surrounding mountains. Orientation of the tombs in the Valley appears to be random, unlike the tombs of the earlier Dynasties at Thebes, which tend to face east; the topographical and geological structure of the Valley assures that this could never be practically achieved for all tombs. However, Tomb KV 39 with its entrance facing east like the earlier Theban tombs, seems a strong candidate for Amenophis I. This theory is in direct conflict with the view held by Howard Carter, who was convinced that the tomb of Amenophis I was AN B situated outside the Valley of the Kings at Dra Abu el-Naga, the site of the royal cemetery of the XVIIth Dynasty.[10] Reeves discusses the burial of Amenophis I and the

---

[1] The re-clearance of the unidentified Theban Tomb KV39, supported by Pacific Western University was carried out over five seasons: September/October 1989; November/December 1991; October/November 1992; September/October 1993; September 1994. Dr John Rose was the Field Director during this period and the work of clearing KV 39 was undertaken in successive seasons by a team of Gurna workmen.
[2] Thomas 1966, 98, n54.
[3] Thomas 1966, 74.
[4] Weigall 1910, 223 ff.
[5] Weigall 1911, 12, 174-5.
[6] Rose 2000, 151.
[7] Papyrus Abbott (BM EA 10221): Peet 1930, pl. 1.

[8] Rose 2000, 16.
[9] Reeves 1996, 88.
[10] Carter 1914, 147-54.

ownership of these two tombs, which have been variously ascribed to this Pharaoh and comes to the conclusion that Carter's tomb at Dra Abu el-Naga is the one most likely to be described in Papyrus Abbott.[11]

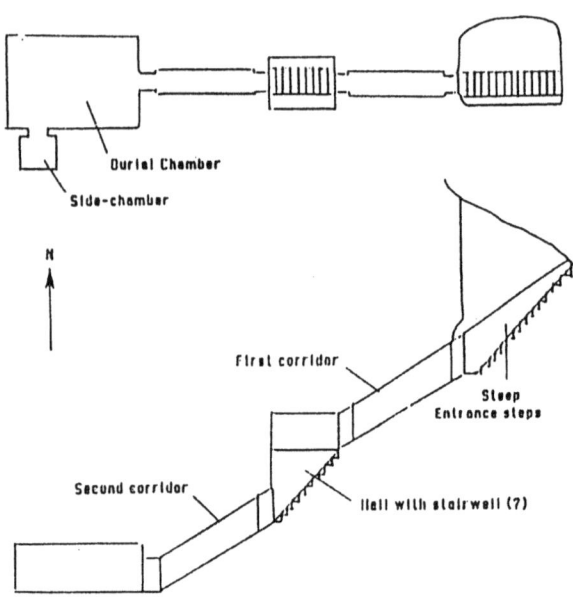

Fig. 1. Plan of KV 39 as envisaged by Elizabeth Thomas. After Thomas 1966.

In contrast Schmitz,[12] on the basis of later textual sources, identifies TT320 in the valley of Deir el-Bahri as the original tomb of the King. More recently, Polz proffers the view: "that all pAbbott based attempts to identify the tomb of Amenhotep I over the last nearly 100 years have yielded close to nothing; the alleged tombs of the king are scattered throughout the necropolis from Dra Abu el-Naga in the north east and the valley of Deir el-Bahri, to the Valley of the Kings in the South West."[13] A conjectural plan and section had been drawn up and published in 1966 by Thomas (see fig. 1), but was based partly on conjecture, from descriptions given by Weigall and Mrs Smith, since Thomas found the tomb sealed by a large rock prior to 1966. [14]The tomb had long since been plundered and never properly excavated. When the full facts from the on-going archaeological excavation from tomb KV 39 are known, the writer may be able to make a more convincing case for KV 39 being the original tomb of Amenophis I. The quest was to solve the riddle of the double enigma – what was the layout of the tomb and more intriguingly for whom was it built?

Description and plan of the tomb

The Pacific Western University Mission started its archaeological investigation and re-clearance of KV39 in September 1989. The amount of debris left by the original excavators took up considerable space around the tomb site making the surface very uneven and it was necessary partially to clear this in order to make safe working access to the entrance. The tomb had been blocked for many years as a large rock had fallen from the *gebel* into the stairwell and it was necessary to break and remove it before the well could be cleared and the tomb entered. The entrance stairwell itself was completely full of detritus to above 7 m (see fig. 2). Subsequently, an archaeological clearance of the interior of tomb KV39 was made in order to establish the exact plan and elevations of the tomb and in the process numerous fragmentary objects were discovered. The tomb doorway and entrance passage way were almost completely blocked with debris, but there was sufficient space to allow access over the top to make an evaluation of other parts of the tomb. The interior of the tomb had fallen victim to the ravages of time and was half full of debris to the extent that in no area could the original floor be seen. Corridors, halls and chambers contained flood debris – rock and fractured shale together with other material - but none of the remaining walls displayed any inscriptions. The tomb's architecture was slowly uncovered as signs of early XVIIIth Dynasty construction was noticed. This dating is further supported by the fact that there is no protective well in the tomb, and therefore it is reasonable to conclude that KV 39 was constructed earlier than the tomb of Tuthmosis III. The first season's work revealed that the tomb layout was significantly different from the original descriptions of the tomb given by Weigall, Smith and the plan envisaged by Thomas. A revised schematic plan of the tomb (see fig. 3) was presented in season 1993 and this remains unchanged.

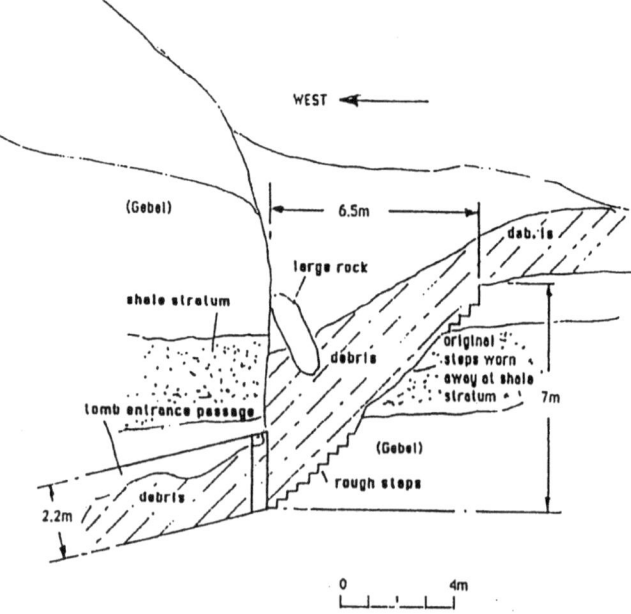

Fig. 2. Schematic section plan of the entrance to KV 39. Reproduced from Rose 2000.

---

[11] Reeves 1990, 3 ff.
[12] Schmitz 1978, 205-32.
[13] Polz 1995, 13.
[14] Thomas 1966, 85, Fig. 9.

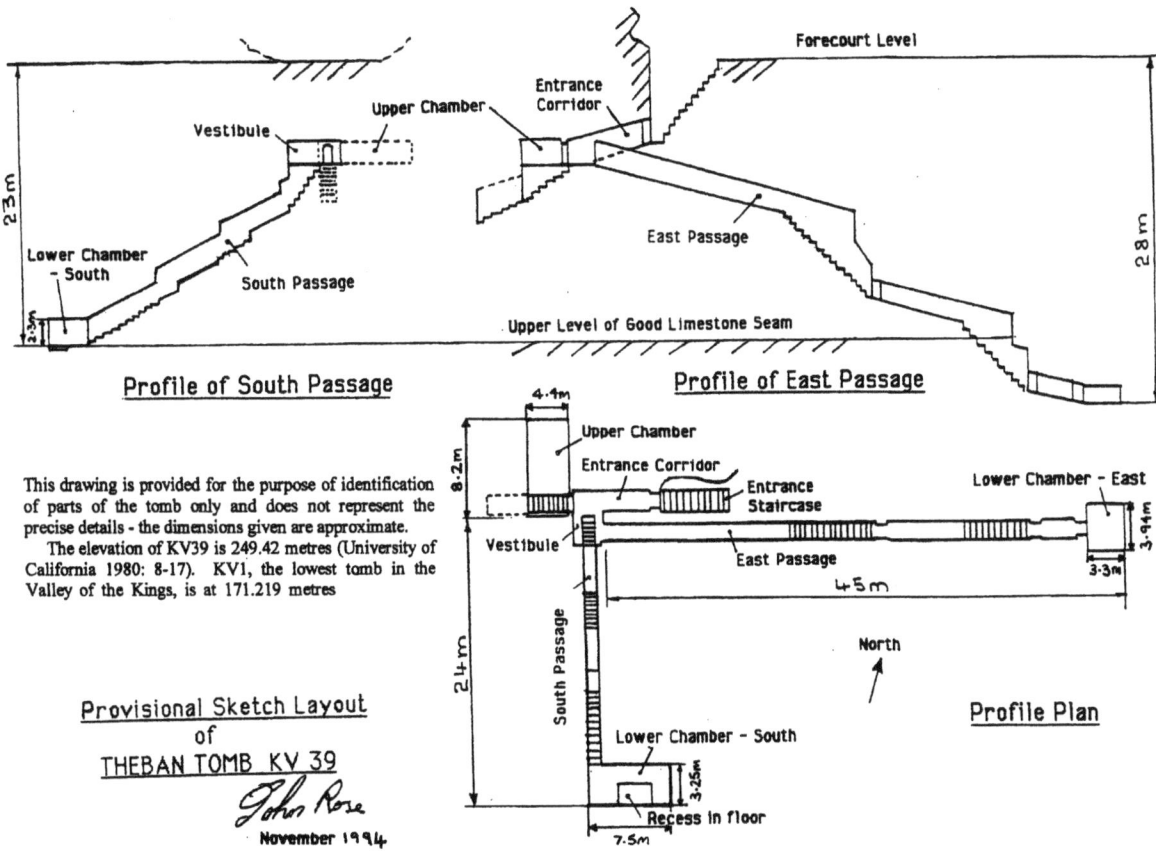

Fig. 3. Tomb plan (1994) of KV 39. Reproduced from Rose 2000.

Upper Chamber, East Passage and Southern Passage

The tombs of the XVIIIth Dynasty in the Valley were of new design, fairly short, with the Burial Chamber offset to the entrance. Those who were responsible for the construction of tomb KV 39 cut vertically into a massive white/cream, well-jointed limestone, which forms the natural surface rock of this part of the Valley. It is into this limestone section that the vestibule and the entrances to the East and South passages were hewn out and in the lowest level of which the Upper Chamber is entirely constructed. A series of steps have been dug on the south side of the Upper Chamber to a depth of 2.6 m. The steps end in a natural rock wall, and do not appear to lead to any other man-made feature, but require further investigation.

Inside the well-cut Upper Chamber are two entrances to descending passages. The East Passage, the largest, begins at 180 degrees to the entrance passage and descends very steeply into the Burial Chamber and floor of the wadi. The East Passage walls have been carefully hewn in most parts, about 2 m wide and extends some 45 m, terminating in a rough flight of steps before a skilfully chiselled doorway 1.7 m wide with jams 1 m thick. Beyond is a 3.5 m long horizontal passage, at the end of which is another fine doorway leading into a chamber 3.3 m x 3.9 m which was almost full of *turab*. In the floor of the chamber there are two joint planes, which appear to have formed a good drainage point for the tomb. Architectural features and cutting techniques found in the tomb entrance, East Passage and Burial Chamber are characteristic of the early XVIIIth Dynasty.[15] The entrance to the South Passage begins in the floor of the Upper Chamber and slopes down steeply through limestone, which becomes progressively more marly, more fractured and unlike the East Passage with no natural drainage features in the Burial Chamber. The limestone walls are extremely soft, porous and uneven. The flood debris had set like concrete, but within this matrix at all levels were fragmented tomb objects. For example, In the Burial Chamber a skeletal hand was discovered in the debris. Fractured shale saturated with water made the whole wall like plaster, which had slumped down over the hand. The hand appeared when the debris was cleared. The rough construction of the South Passage and Chamber, which extends some 24 m, suggests either a design for a cache or an unfinished tomb. The dimensions of the South Chamber are approximately 7.5 m long x 3.2 m wide x 2.3 m high. There is a recess set in the floor adjacent to the south wall – this recess is 1.65 m wide times 3 m long x 0.2 m deep (see fig. 3). Reeves' view is that this cut in the floor was intended to receive a coffin, which was "reminiscent of

---

[15] Romer 1992, *pers. com.*

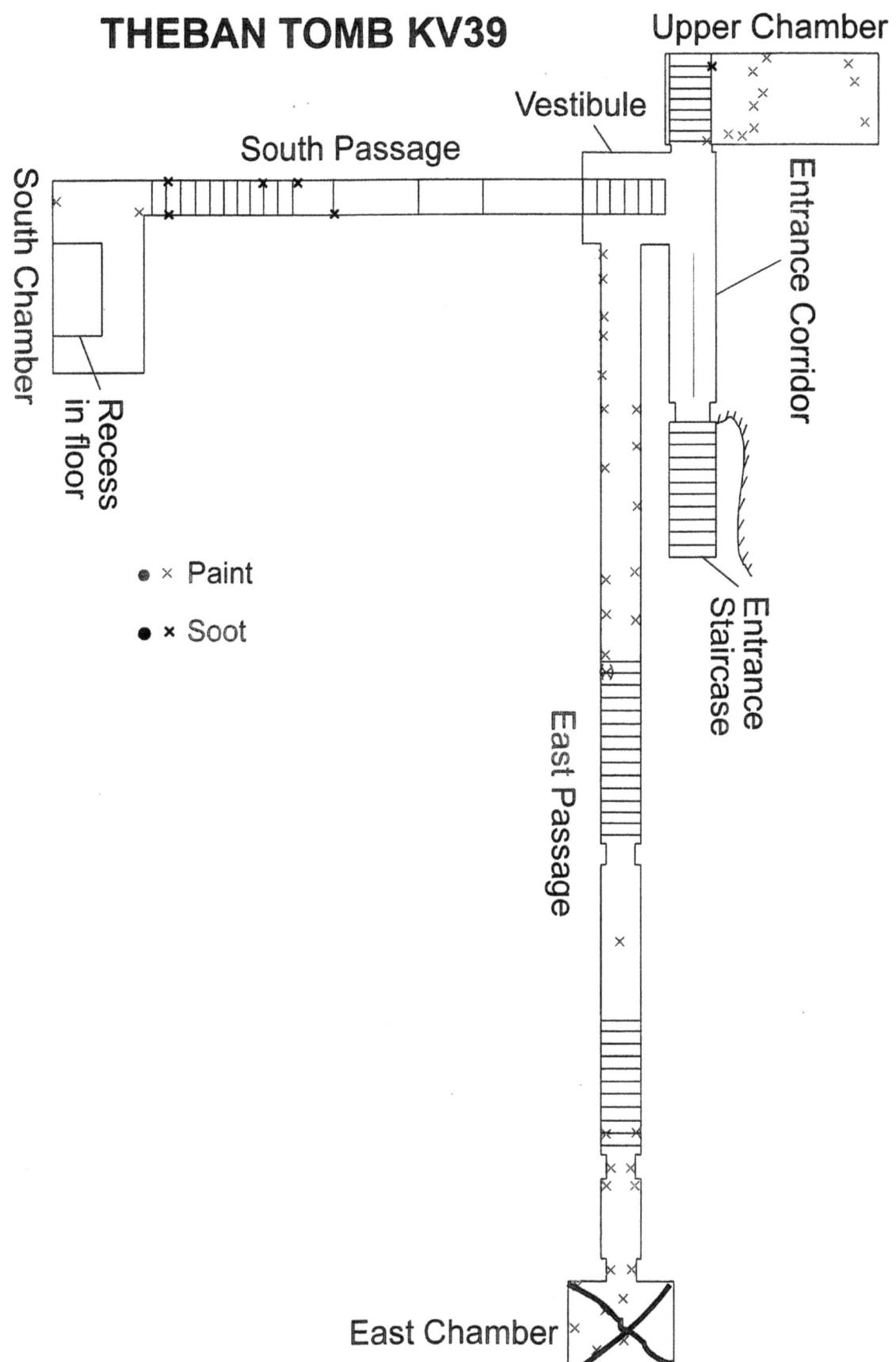

Fig. 4. Schematic plan by Dr Stephen Buckley.

pre New Kingdom sepulchres".[16] A grid of red paint markers on the ceiling of the Upper Chamber and walls of the East Passage clearly indicated the tomb-builders' guidelines (see fig. 4) but there was an absence of inscriptions. At the end of each season the tomb was sealed and a stone razza built to prevent ingress of dust and water.

Selected Finds

The clearance of KV 39 has revealed some datable material deriving from the early to middle of the XVIIIth Dynasty, which are detailed below, together with other selected finds. However, the writer wishes to point out that a large number of fragments of various objects were recovered during the course of clearance of the tomb, some of which are briefly listed under '*other fragments*' in their respective tomb locations of discovery and might, importantly, contain objects from the original burial; tomb robbers would probably not be interested in 'day-to-day' pottery sherds for example.

From the clearance of the Courtyard and Entrance

Eight-sandstone dockets[17]
The dockets bear cartouches in blue paint giving the prenomens tentatively identified as the pharaohs of the early XVIIIth Dynasty i.e. Aakheperkare (Tuthmosis I), Aakheperenre (Tuthmosis II (?)) and Aakheperure (Amenophis II) the purpose of which is not yet clear. Dodson likens them to dummy grinding stones found in temple foundation deposits.[18]

Mud seals with hieroglyph impressions[19]
Depicting a cartouche with plurality strokes, which can only relate to Amenophis II or, less likely, Tuthmosis IV.

None of the eight-sandstone dockets or the mud seals with hieroglyphics indicate tomb ownership but they suggest that the tomb was connected with royalty.

Two limestone Ostraca, each inscribed with five lines of cursive hieroglyphs[20]

The two ostraca are identified by Quirke "as fragments from a funerary ritual, and perhaps specifically as drafts for a scene to be represented on the walls of the tomb".[21] It has also been suggested that the titles may relate to some of the 'guests' attending the funeral with old, established priestly titles, having been invited or requested to serve in their particular priestly role.[22] The priestly titles depicted include 'lector priest', 'master of ceremonies', 'great one of the god', 'king's sculpture and (priest) who is in the palace chamber', 'master of the great', 'servant of the earth', 'the builder great indeed'.

A small piece of alabaster (calcite)
This is slightly tapered, truncated form, 3.5cm by 3.0cm, possibly the base of a miniature vessel.

A group of small ceramic vessels
Vessels both complete and broken, comprising bowls, jars and cups from foundation deposit.

The remains of a mummified bird or food offering
The mummification process applied may be dated in future work.

Cordage
Some possibly associated with the tomb builders.

Organic matter including seeds in pouches
Probably intended to sustain life in the next world.

A small limestone-offering table
Found at the outside entrance to the tomb.

Four bronze tools
Likely used by the workmen cutting the tomb or part of a foundation deposit.

OTHER FRAGMENTS

A fragment of pottery with ankh sign.

A large corpus of ceramic fragments.

Fragments of coloured plaster.

Two flakes of gold leaf.

An agate bead and an agate peg.

A faience bead, a chip of blue faience.

There were numerous hazards encountered during the excavation.[23]

Finds from sieving the external original excavator's dump

A bronze/gold signet ring[24]
On the bezel of which are hieroglyphic signs that read the name of Menkheperre (Tuthmosis III). Though its identification as a working ring, used as a seal (it could

---

[16] Reeves 1996, 89.
[17] Rose 2000, pl. 35.
[18] Dodson 2003 *pers com*; c.f., UC28828, an 18th Dynasty sandstone model grindstone in the Petrie Museum of Egyptian Archaeology.
[19] Rose 2000, pl. 30.
[20] Rose 2000, pl. 27.
[21] Quirke 2001, *pers. com.*
[22] Kitchen 2001, *pers. com.*

[23] One hazard of clearing this area was the emergence of two snakes, probably male and female, in successive seasons – not really surprising for the mountain is called after Meretseger, the snake goddess – 'she who loves silence!'
[24] Rose 2000, pl. 59.

certainly be used as one) may be valid, the possibility remains of it being a valued piece of jewellery. This discovery can add fuel to the theory of the tomb being used in the Osirification of the royal mummies prior to them being eventually re-located in the royal cache. The signet ring could simply have dislodged from the finger of the mummy during the re-embalming process, thus recording its transportation to KV 39 before being taken to the Deir el-Bahri cache.

Fragment of an alabaster jar[25]
This piece is probably part of a calcite (alabaster) canopic jar since it has a vertical column of blue hieroglyphs beginning with the word Osiris i.e., the deceased. The column is incomplete, the lower portion, which is missing, probably containing the jar owner's name; an uninscribed matching piece of the jar was recovered from the lower steps leading to the South Passage Burial Chamber. Both these pieces include part of the rim. The inscribed fragment has the title: 'Osiris, steward, Amen', the Amen being followed by a central blue dot, which appears to be the centrally disposed tip of the next hieroglyph. The complete name of this person is missing. The sign for 'hotep' is one that is so centrally disposed and is certainly a possibility. The title denotes a person of high office and an inscribed alabaster jar such as this is usually from a funerary context and is therefore very likely to be near the original tomb.

However, the last word could be the god Amen. The writing of the period permitted the name of the god to be written with or without the determinative hieroglyph for a god (the seated figure). The remaining fragment of the sign following Amen could be the top of the head of this figure, in either case, therefore, the last word could be the god Amen.[26]

Many items bear fragmentary inscriptions, invaluable information but never quite sufficient to provide the conclusive piece of evidence in identifying the tomb owner.

OTHER FRAGMENTS

A large corpus of ceramic fragments.

A large number of fragments of wooden objects.

Fragment of mummy cloth.

Fragment of limestone offering table.

Flakes of gold leaf.

A few faience beads.

A small pouch

From clearance of the Upper Chamber, East Passage and Southern Passage

Fragments of wooden coffins[27]
These include pieces with yellow paintwork on a black background and some with hieroglyphic signs painted yellow on black background – the signs in sunken relief, the earliest examples of which are datable to the end of the first decade of Tuthmosis III's reign.[28] This datable evidence perhaps indicates secondary burials.

Fragments from a coffin lid
These were of different colours indicating perhaps the presence of more than one coffin.

Mummy cloth from East Passage
A plentiful supply of mummy bandages of different grades and a quantity of embalmers' pouches or swabs led to the conjecture about the use of the tomb as a re-wrapping place.

Skeletal remains
There were at least nine bodies buried in the tomb, not necessarily all from the same period. A minimum of three from the Upper Chamber, two or three from the Burial Chamber, East Passage and four or five from the Lower chamber, South Passage. The Burial Chamber, East Passage, appears to contain a particularly important burial, judging by the quality of finds from this area. A skull in particular was of a high standard of mummification. From a sample of resin taken off one of the mummies methyl 7-oxodehydroabieatate was found to be present (c. 5%) in Resin B3. This confirms the practice of mummification on at least this body and importantly the use of coniferous resin as part of the embalming process.[29] Evidently, the Egyptians had access to the coniferous resins and their sources, but was the coniferous resin supplied and applied in c.1500 B.C.? Since coniferous resins were not native to Egypt, this may have important implications for trade routes and dating, given the tomb was allegedly built shortly after the expulsion of the Hyksos, at the beginning of the New Kingdom. It might be expected that trade routes in the Near East (where coniferous trees were likely to be found) would be difficult to establish and maintain at this time. In the philosophical tract 'The Admonitions of Ipuwer', the lamentations of the author include the situation in which "*Men do not sail to Byblos today. What can we do to get Cedars for our mummies? Priests are buried with their produce, and Princes are embalmed with their resin, as far as the land of Keftiu, and now they come no more*".[30] Although the piece is set in an earlier period, Lichtheim herself in the introduction to it says it must be "late Middle Kingdom".[31] This evidence raises

---

[25] Rose 2000, pl. 53.
[26] Rose 2000, *pers. com.*

[27] Rose 2000, pl. 38.
[28] Dodson 2003, 187-93.
[28] Buckley 2000.
[29] Erman 1978, 96.
[30] Alternative reading Lichtheim 1975, 152.

the question again of were the mummies then of later date? On the other hand, coniferous resin can be stockpiled; the earliest firm evidence for the storage/burial of large amounts of a coniferous resin or (cedar or pine-chemical analysis was not able to identify in order the exact type of resin) was found mixed with oil/fat in a range of storage jars in the First Dynasty tomb of Djer at Abydos.[32] Detailed examination by an anthropologist may reveal dates, ages and resemblances and ultimately assist in identifying the tomb owner. Further study of the mummy cloth by a textile specialist may also provide supporting evidence for confirmation of dates.[33]

Skeletal hand of a child
With traces of mummification.

A skull
With traces of mummification.

A wooden false beard
Giving an indication of the status of the tomb owner.

A small wooden bolt
From a chest.

A wooden claw foot
From a substantial piece of furniture.

An inlay eye of ivory with an obsidian pupil
From a mask or statue.

Linen pouches containing organic matter
Discovered in the East Passage.

A large number of mud-jar sealings
These were discovered in the Burial Chamber at the bottom of the East Passage. The underside of one has a light brown/beige painted surface and clearly shows the imprint from the reeds binding the jar stopper. The painted surface is intended to render the mud non-porous and thus prevent the contents (in this case probably wine) from evaporating.

Pieces of plaited hair and other hair wig curls[34]
Careful examination of the hair remains is required by a specialist in order to determine the nature of the samples i.e. date, mode and purpose. Importantly, Fletcher points out that *"Although plaits are quite common throughout the dynastic period, they seem to be particular popular on bodies/remains dated to the second Intermediate Period and early XVIIIth Dynasty"*.[35] I should mention that there is a description of the plaited hair that Carter found in Qurna tomb-37.[36]

---

[32] Serpico and White 1996, 128-39.
[34] Fletcher 2001, *pers. com.*
[33] Fletcher 2001, *pers. com.*
[34] Rose 2000, pl. 57.
[35] Fletcher 2001, *pers. com.*
[36] Carnarvon and Carter 1912, 85.

Other fragments

Fragment of large pottery jars containing mummified remains

Fragments of very thick-walled alabaster vessels

A large number of fragments of thick walled pottery

Flakes of gold

Summary

The tomb seems to have three separate sections, probably added on to the original basic design. Romer argues that the tomb architecture and the chisel marks, found near the door jambs in the East Passage, are early XVIIIth Dynasty; the architecture is undecorated and devoid of inscriptions. The rough construction of the South Passage suggests either a design for a cache or an unfinished tomb. There are a number of different scenarios to explain the condition of KV 39 as it was found but from the very large quantities of mummy cloth and pottery sherds found in the East Passage in season 1991 it would seem that robbers had plundered the Burial Chamber, dragging out the coffins, smashing them and destroying the mummies, leaving the coffin pieces and smashed pottery scattered along the floor of the passage. These items seemed to have been covered over, perhaps by later flood debris and by rock and shale fragments falling from the walls and ceilings. The problem is that in this case we were not able to account for or to date with any certainty the subsequent derangement caused by human activities in the archaeological context. Difficulties are compounded by the fact that it is still unresolved as to what prerequisites prevailed for other persons to be interred subsequently in the tomb of the supposed tomb owner.

The majority of bodies were of tall males with possibly a shorter male or female and an even smaller male or female. This could suggest a family burial with a later cache and a detailed study of the skeletal remains could establish family ties and importantly whether or not they are from the same period. The reasonably clear name of Amenophis II on one of the cartouches found on the blue dockets certainly raises the question (as does the mud seal with the plurality sign) of a measure of involvement of KV 39 with Amenophis II, members of his family or person(s) serving that Pharaoh. Indeed the inscribed objects mentioned above represent high quality evidence, particularly those that may eventually be identifiable as belonging to the tomb-users. Whilst the architecture of KV 39 indicates early XVIIIth Dynasty, the turmoil of re-burials, usurpations (illegal acts) and items of datable evidence warrants extension of the period to be considered for dating conjectured successive ownership of the tomb, at least until the middle of the New Kingdom.[37]

Future work

Nature of the proposed work: this coming season further investigation and clearance is required in the area of the steps in the Upper Chamber. Overall measurement of the tomb has been undertaken but a final architectural survey should be made. This will allow the final plan to be produced. The sieving of the original excavators' dump was continued in the last season and requires to be systematically completed. Final specialist study of pottery, skeletal, textile, hair and other organic materials and further research of existing finds should allow completion of the project.

Acknowledgments

On behalf of the team I would like to express our thanks to the Committee of the Egyptian Antiquities Organisation (EAO) for granting permission to carry out the project, in particular to the Chairman Dr Sayed Tawfiq and the Supervisor for Upper Egypt, Mr Mutaua Balbush. Our thanks also go to the Director General for Luxor, Dr Mohammedel-Sughayer, the Director of el-Qurna, Dr Mohammed Nasr and other members of the EAO at Luxor and el-Qurna, whose help is very much appreciated. I am grateful for recent discussions I have had with colleagues, especially Ashley Cooke, Dr Aidan Dodson, Professor Kenneth Kitchen, Dr Steven Snape, Dr Stephen Quirke and Dr Penny Wilson.

Ian M. Buckley
The University of Liverpool

Cited Works

Carnavon, G.H. and Carter, H.
    1912 *Five Years' Exploration at Thebes. A Record of Work Done 1907-1911* London: H. Frowde
Carter, H.
    1914 'Report on the tomb of Zeser-ka-ra Amenhotep I, discovered by the Earl of Carnarvon in 1914', *JEA 3: 147-54*
Dodson, A.
    2003 'The Burial of Members of the Royal Family During the Eighteenth Dynasty', in Z. Hawass and L. Pinch Brock (eds.), Egyptology at the dawn of the twenty-first century: proceedings of the Eighth International Congress of Egyptologists, vol. 2. Cairo: American University in Cairo Press, 2003, 187-93.

Erman, A.
    1978 *The Ancient Egyptians: a Sourcebook of their Writings*, A. M. Blackman (trans.) Gloucester: Peter Smith.
Lichtheim, M.
    1975 *Ancient Egyptian Literature: Volume 1: The Old and Middle Kingdoms*. London: University of California Press
Peet, T.E.
    1930 *The Great Tomb-Robberies of the Twentieth Egyptian Dynasty*. Oxford: Clarendon
Poltz, D.
    1995 'The Location of the Tomb of Amenhotep I: A Reconsideration', in Wilkinson, R. H. (ed.) *Valley of the Sun Kings – New Explorations in the Tombs of the Pharaohs*. Tucsan: The University of Arizona Egyptian Expedition
Reeves, C.N.
    1990 *Valley of the Kings: The Decline of the Royal Necropolis*. London: Keegan Paul International
Reeves, C.N. and R.H. Wilkinson
    1996 *The Complete Valley of the Kings - Tombs and Treasures of Egypt's Greatest Pharaohs*. London: Thames and Hudson Ltd
Rose, J.
    2000 *Tomb KV39 In the Valley of the Kings – A Double Archaeological Enigma*. Bristol: Western Academic and Specialist Press Ltd
Schmitz, F. J.
    1978 'Amenophis I', *HÄB 6:205-32*
Serpico, M. and White, R.
    1996 A Report on the Analysis of the Contents of a Cache of Jars from the Tomb of Djer, *Aspects of Early Egypt*, J. Spencer (ed.). London: British Museum Press
Thomas, E.
    1966 *The Royal Necropoleis of Thebes*. Princeton (NJ): Princeton University Press
Weigall, A. E. P.
    1910 *A Guide to the Antiquities of Upper Egypt*. London: Thornton Butterworth
    1911 'The tomb of Amenhotep', *ASAE II: 12, 174-75*.

---

[37] Carnarvon and Carter 1912, 85.

An Old Kingdom Town at Zawiet Sultan (Zawiet Meitin) in Middle Egypt: A Preliminary Report

Nadine Moeller

Introduction

The remains of the once prominent pharaonic settlement called Hebenu, which was the capital of the 16th Upper Egyptian nome, can be located near the modern village of Zawiet Sultan. It is also often mentioned in connection with Zawiet el-Meitin ("region of the dead"), which refers to the large modern cemetery east of Zawiet Sultan. These places are situated on the east bank of the Nile about 15 km south-east of El Minya in Middle Egypt. The settlement area today is characterised by large heaps of broken pottery and some remains of mud-brick structures mainly dating to Graeco-Roman times. This destruction of the site was caused by the sebakhin who were digging for fertilizer from the middle of the last century until the 1930s. Aerial photographs show numerous burial shafts stretching along the desert slope, which have been mostly robbed. In December 1999 and 2000 members of the Inspectorate of Antiquities of Minya and Universities of Cambridge and Sheffield carried out an archaeological survey at this settlement site. This project is under the direction of Mahmud Hamza, Barry Kemp and Paul Buckland.

General description of the site (fig.1)

About 90 per cent of the pottery scattered on the surface dates to Graeco-Roman times. Remains of mud-brick walls, parts of olive presses and sections of a large enclosure wall indicate that a substantial settlement occupied the area during that period. Foundations of a small stone temple are exposed at the southern end of the site possibly dating similarly (fig. 1) which also demonstrate the large extent of the settlement. Remnants of a New Kingdom temple dedicated to "Horus, Lord of Hebenu" were found in the northern part of the site (fig.1). In this area stone blocks inscribed with the cartouches of Amenophis III and Ramesses III were discovered. Further evidence for New Kingdom activities is found in some rock tombs in the cliffs above the temple, the best known of which is the tomb of Nefersekheru.[1]

There are also some Old Kingdom remains visible at the site. One of the earliest structures is a small step pyramid, which is situated in the northern part of the site (fig.1). The sides are about 20 m long and it probably had three

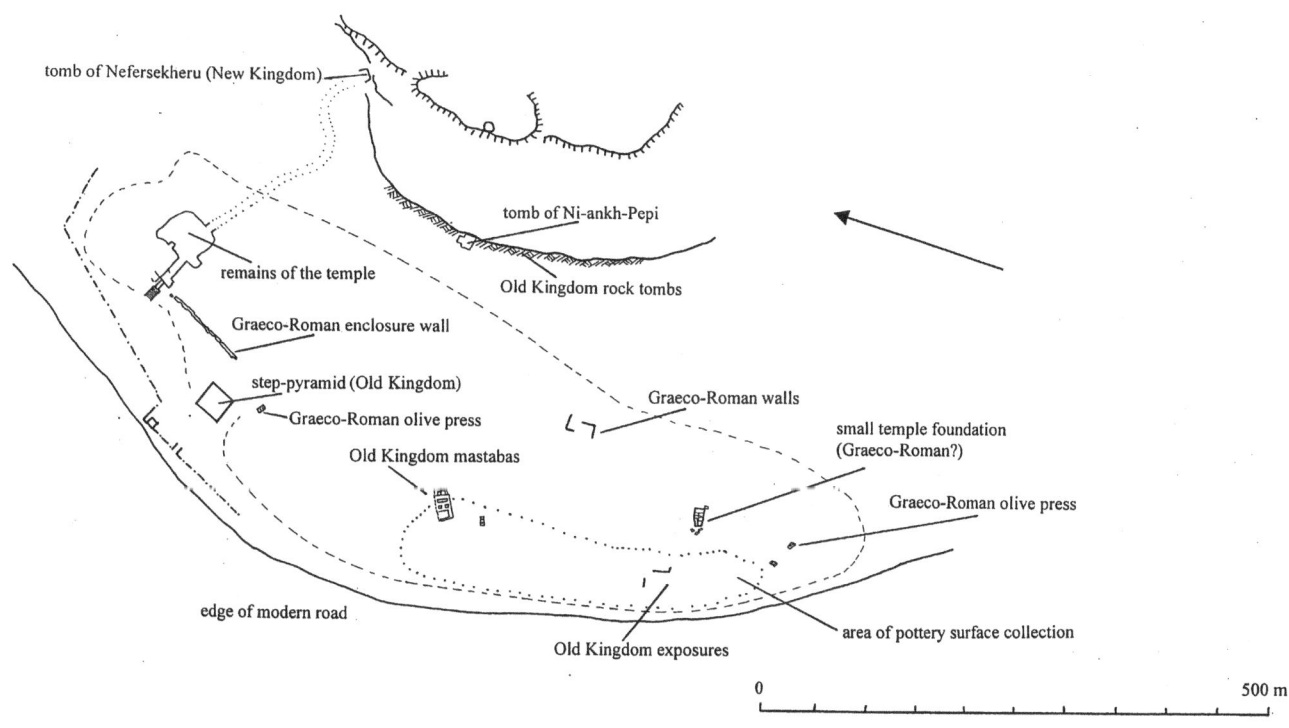

Fig. 1. Sketch map of the site of ancient Hebenu near Zawiet Sultan.

---

[1] Osing 1992.

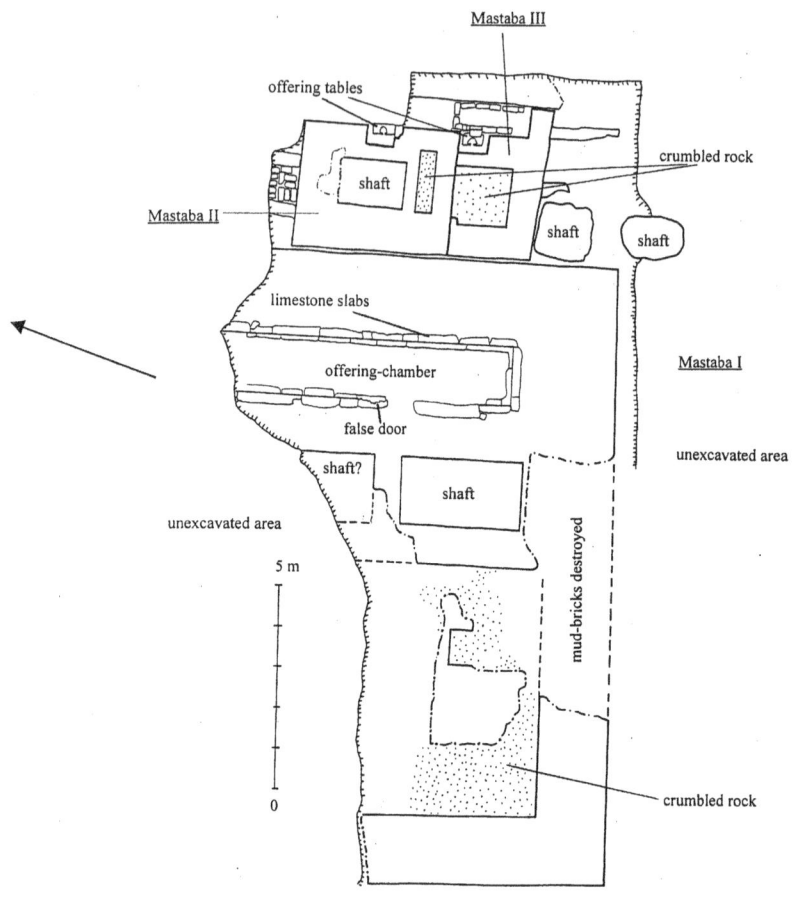

Fig. 2. Old Kingdom Mastabas

arrangement can be found at the cemetery of Beni Hasan.[4] Some Old Kingdom mastaba tombs situated further downhill and therefore close to the settlement area were discovered during recent fieldwork carried out at the site. Furthermore, two building complexes dating to the same period were located about 300 m southwest of the mastaba-tombs (fig.1). These discoveries provide important new information about the history and development of Hebenu.

The mastaba-tombs (fig.2)

Three mastaba tombs were discovered in an area 200 m south of the pyramid (fig. 1). A stone-lined "room" was first visible among loose unstratified debris that consists mainly of Graeco-Roman sherds and rubble. These heaps of debris limited the area of the excavation to an irregular strip, measuring roughly 10 by 20 m, which ran steeply downhill.

The stone-lined "room" turned out to be an offering-chamber belonging to a mastaba tomb. After clearing the rubble and sherds away three mastaba tombs of different sizes became visible (fig. 2). The offering-chamber belongs to the largest tomb, termed Mastaba I. It lies on the eastern side and was originally situated inside its superstructure, which was made of mud-bricks. Only this offering chamber contained stone elements. It had been lined with slabs of limestone varying between 15 and 25 cm in thickness. The limestone slabs around the sides stand on a narrow plinth of stone, which probably marks the edge of a stone floor, which has been lost. Two false doors were situated on the western wall of this chamber, of which the smaller one is still *in situ* (fig. 2). The larger one was lying on the ground and originally stood in the adjacent gap. Their surfaces are too worn to trace any inscriptions. The northern part of the mastaba was not cleared and is still buried underneath a huge pile of rubble and sherds. Two shafts are situated behind the false doors, towards the west (fig. 2). The northern one is still partially buried under the rubble and will be cleared in the next season. The southern shaft is filled with Graeco-Roman sherds and rubble and it is therefore likely that it was robbed by the *sebakhin*. A complete clearance of this shaft will be undertaken in the future. The western face of the western wall of the shafts bore mud-plaster indicating that it once

to four steps. Its exterior had a casing of limestone blocks. There are no burial chambers inside or underneath it. This pyramid presumably had only a symbolic function. According to its architecture it can be dated to the late 3rd / early 4th Dynasty.[2] A line of rock-tombs, which were built for the higher officials during the 5th and early 6th Dynasties are cut into the cliffs overlooking the site (fig.1). Nowadays only limited information can be gained from them because they were severely damaged and partially destroyed by quarrying activities, which happened after Lepsius planned and copied them.[3] The tomb of Ni-ankh-Pepi is the only one that can still be visited today. Underneath these rock-cut tombs, on a broad desert slope, a large number of tomb shafts can be seen. Some of them had fragments and few complete Old Kingdom beer jars and other characteristic pottery scattered around the shaft. They presumably all date to the Old Kingdom too. The Graeco-Roman settlement was built partially over them. The *sebakh*-digging exposed them again and probably during that time they were robbed. These tomb shafts belong to the less wealthy officials and their families. A close parallel for such an

---

[2] Dreyer and Kaiser 1980, 43-59.
[3] Lepsius 1904, 57-69

[4] Garstang 1907.

formed the outside of the mastaba. Against it, however, was banked a deposit of loose, crumbly marl dug from the desert which the builders had used as fill in parts of this mastaba. This points to the likelihood that the superstructure was enlarged further to the west and that the prominent corner in the western part of the excavations is the actual south-west corner of the tomb (fig. 2). Here the internal parts are partially destroyed and thus difficult to interpret. It might be possible that this extension was used for further burials, but up to now clear evidence of any shafts is missing. Mastaba I may have been originally built for two people, presumably a married couple. The southern, larger false door would then belong to the burial of the husband, a tradition which is well known from mastabas of the court-cemeteries.[5] The extension towards the west might have contained further burials of family members. These burials may have been incorporated into the superstructure of the mastaba, which would explain the lack of additional shafts in this area.[6]

The offering-chamber is constructed as a corridor within the mud-brick superstructure of the mastaba. This type of offering chamber developed from 2nd and 3rd Dynasty tombs, which can be seen, for example, at mastabas found at Naga-ed-Deir[7] where the offering-places were enclosed by a low wall and thus formed an open corridor. Sometimes a wall surrounding the whole mastaba led to a similar layout. This tradition continued during the later Old Kingdom. With mastabas of the 5th and 6th Dynasty at Giza the lack of space between the tomb structures resulted in such a corridor construction.[8] The tomb of Ni-ka-ankh[9] at Tehna, a cemetery site that lies about 20 km north of Zawiet Sultan on the east bank, has a very similar offering chamber compared to Mastaba I. Although Ni-ka-ankh's tomb was cut into the cliffs, the layout resembles closely that of a mastaba.[10] A corridor has been cut around a rectangular rock-core, which on the eastern side leads into an offering-chamber that has the form of a corridor. Two false doors are situated on its western side behind which a crude shaft was created. This construction is the closest parallel to Mastaba I.

On the eastern side of Mastaba I, at the top of the slope, two further mastabas of much smaller size were discovered. One of them, termed Mastaba II, has a complete plan and was built against the east face of Mastaba I. It measures 4 by 3 metres and is subdivided into two compartments. The narrower on the south was filled with pale, crumbly, desert marl. The larger one, which was destroyed to its foundations, seems to be the upper part of a tomb shaft. On account of the limited time available the shaft was not excavated this season. On the eastern side of Mastaba II an intact offering-table was found. It is decorated with a Hetep-hieroglyph flanked by two small basins. On the south side stood the lower part of a stone-lined niche, which presumably contained a false door at the rear. The rear vertical edge of the jamb bore a slight lip, showing where it would have joined the rear slab of the niche. Against its southern side a third mastaba (Mastaba III) was built. The square space in the centre, which was surrounded by mud-bricks, contained desert marl and there was no indication of a shaft. Probably a shaft was intended here but left unfinished, or the burial was integrated into the superstructure of the tomb instead of being placed in a shaft. On its eastern side another intact offering-table was found very similar to the one from Mastaba II. The strong resemblance of this construction with that of Mastaba II suggests that they were built both within roughly the same period of time. Next to it on the southern side two more shafts were discovered but have not yet been excavated. Two mud-brick walls running in a right angle to Mastaba III might indicate further structures, which were partially destroyed by the *sebakhin*. The façade of Mastabas II and III bore a thick, slightly orange coloured plaster of which traces are still visible. Within the rubble-filling of Mastaba II a small offering-basin was found, which shows traces of inscription. The cartouche of Merira (Pepi I) can be read which provides a further hint about the date of these mastabas.

The tradition of placing the offering structures on the eastern side of the mastaba is well known from cemeteries at Giza, Saqqara and other west-bank cemeteries.[11] This follows the concept that people coming from the valley would place the offerings for the deceased on the eastern side of the tomb by facing west towards the "land of the deceased". The burial shafts are usually situated behind the false doors and offering-places. This concept becomes problematic when the cemetery is situated on the east bank as it is the case at Zawiet Sultan. Then the valley lies westwards from the tomb and its eastern side faces the cliffs. A comparison with other east bank cemeteries shows that different places came to individual solutions. At the cemetery of Naga ed-Deir tombs were orientated strictly towards the Nile.[12] Therefore the offering-places are on the western side of the mastabas. The orientation to the compass points seemed to have been regarded as secondary in comparison with the concept of orientating the offering places to the valley, the "land of the living". On the other hand, mastabas found in El-Kab[13] have the offering-places on the eastern side similar to the ones at Zawiet Sultan. Furthermore, a mastaba-structure discovered at Cemetery 600 at Mostagedda has a corridor-like structure on its eastern side next to the burial shaft.[14] The excavator dated it to the 6th Dynasty. Only one layer of mud-bricks

---

[5] Reisner 1936, 287.
[6] For such burials within the superstructure, see Seidlmayer 1990, 60-2.
[7] Reisner 1936, 242 fig.127.
[8] Junker 1943, 3, 26 Abb. 3. See also "Übersichtsplan" at the end of the publication.
[9] He was an official during the reign of king Userkaf.
[10] Brunner 1936, 15.

[11] Junker 1943, 3; Seidlmayer 1990, 412.
[12] Mace 1909, pl.58; Reisner 1932, sheet ii.
[13] Quibell 1898, 3, pl.xxiii.
[14] Brunton 1937, 98f.

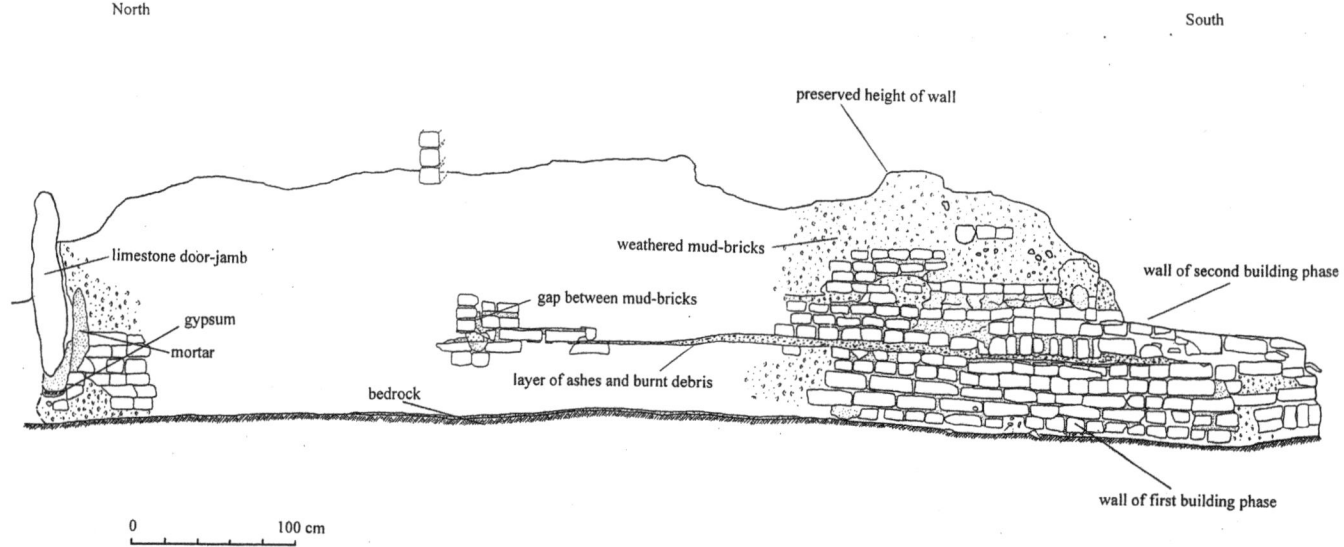

Fig. 3. Old Kingdom exposure 1, west wall.

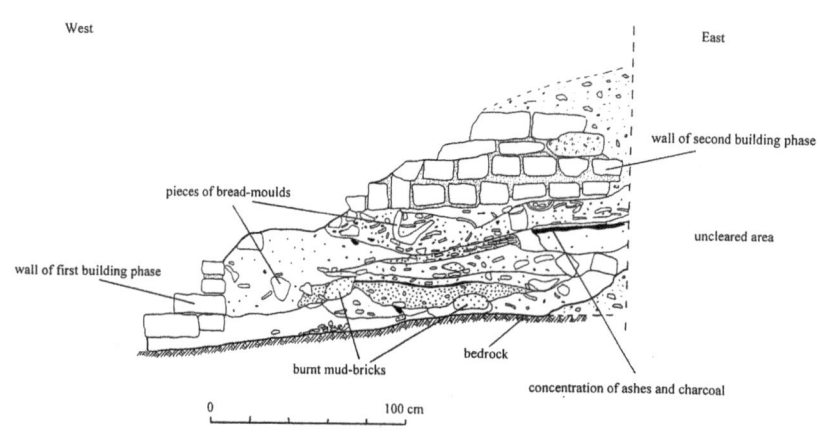

Fig. 4. Old Kingdom exposure 1, south wall.

was preserved and therefore no more detailed information is available. Nevertheless it resembles closely the layout of Mastaba I. The "rock-mastaba" from Tehna, as mentioned above, is another example of a tomb belonging to an east bank cemetery which has its offering chamber on the eastern side. In these cases it seems that it was more important to follow the convention of the Giza/Saqqara tradition than trying to adapt the layout of the tomb structures to the natural landscape.

Along the southern side of Mastaba I a fill consisting of different layers of ashes and debris with numerous red slipped, burnished pieces of pottery including many rims of carinated bowls (so-called "Maidum-bowls") was found along the southern side of Mastaba I (fig. 6). This phenomenon of accumulating debris around a cemetery was also observed at the First Intermediate Period cemetery discovered at Ashmunein.[15] It suggests that this fine ware was used for the offerings, which were brought to the tombs by the family members of the deceased. Pottery will form subject of a future study after further excavations have taken place.

The Old Kingdom settlement at Zawiet Sultan

One part of the survey took place in an area that lies about 300 m south-west of the pyramid (cf. fig. 1). Parts of two building complexes were visible among the heaps of sherds and rubble left from sebakh-digging. The two walls belong to building complexes which can be dated to the Old Kingdom. They are named here *Old Kingdom exposure 1* and *Old Kingdom exposure 2*. Many characteristic Old Kingdom sherds were found lying on the ground around the two walls but also a few diagnostic sherds can be seen within the walls themselves. It seems that the remnants enclosed by these walls belong to the debris left during the Old Kingdom occupation of this area. The ceramic evidence is the main evidence for dating the walls since little stratigraphy has been left intact by sebakh-digging. Rims of carinated bowls (so-

---

[15] Spencer 1993, 53.

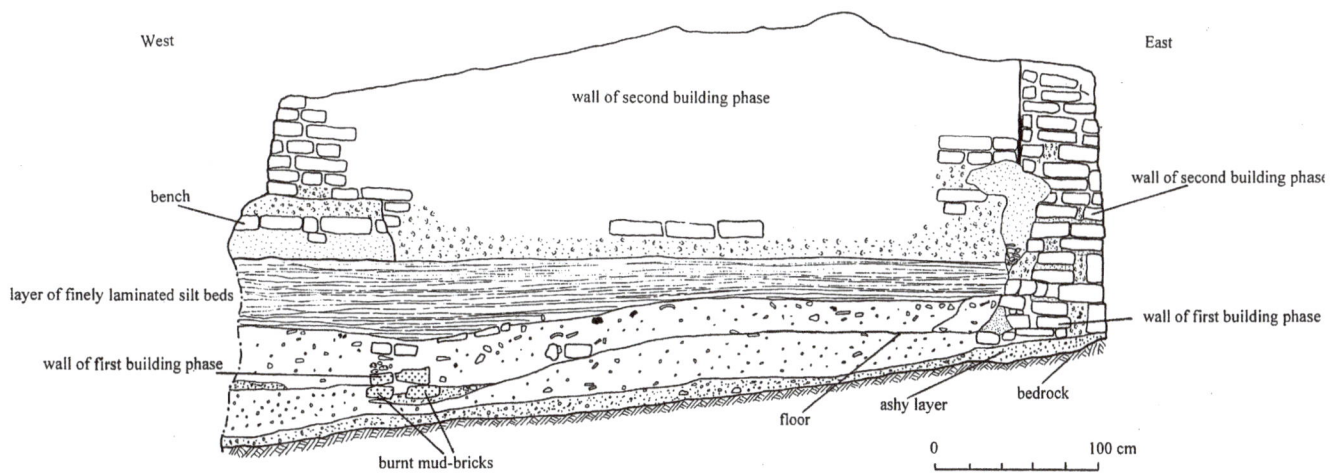

Fig. 5. Old Kingdom exposure 2.

called "Maidum-bowls") and pieces of bread-moulds suggest a late Old Kingdom date for these buildings. *Old Kingdom exposure 1* (fig. 3; pl. I a) consists of two mud-brick walls belonging to a rectangular building. The western wall is about 8.56 m long and it is preserved to a height of between 1.5-1.6 m. A vertical slab of limestone (120 cm high and 12-20 cm thick) is set into the wall at the northern end, resting on a bed of mud and white plaster. It presumably functioned as the jamb of an entrance to this building. The rest of the entrance is still buried underneath sherds and rubble. The southern return wall runs in a right angle to the western wall (fig. 4; pl. I b). It was cleared as far as possible and is now visible for a length of 2.4 m before disappearing into a large heap of sebakh-debris. It had a height of 1.2 m and was built on top of a layer of ashes and debris.

Two building phases can be distinguished. In the earlier phase the west wall was built directly on top of the natural bedrock. At this time the wall extended further to the south, but it is not possible to say how far, because the sebakh digging has destroyed its continuation southwards. The building seems to have been severely affected by fire on its southern part, where thick layer of ashes, charcoal, burnt bricks and pottery accumulated up to a height of 60 cm. The northern part seems to have not been affected by this. The upper part of the west wall was lost and rebuilt later on a thin, ashy layer that covered the stump of the original wall. This implies that the ground outside built up at the same level. This is also confirmed by the southern section (fig. 4; pl. I b): an east-west wall was built on top of this layer containing ashes and burnt debris. During the first building phase the west wall extended further south and there was no east-west wall running in a right angle to it. It is not clear whether this east-west wall formed the new outside wall of the building, enclosing a smaller space than before, or was merely a new inner division wall inside the building changing its internal layout.

The uppermost mud bricks of the west wall show traces of severe erosion, which indicates that the building was exposed to the weather for a long time after its abandonment. They are now covered by sherds and rubble from the Graeco-Roman periods. There are no traces of any settlement in the intervening period. It seems that this part of the town had lain deserted for some two millennia.

The second complex of mud brick walls, *Old Kingdom exposure 2*, lies a few metres north of *Old Kingdom exposure 1*. When first seen it lay surrounded on all four sides by dense sebakh-debris and formed the side of a quarry pit. It was cleared as far as possible, so that the whole wall became clearly visible. In front of it the natural bedrock was reached (fig. 5; pl. II a). The exposed parts of this building complex consist of two walls running at right angles to each other. They form the corner of a building. Here at least two building phases can also be distinguished: the lower part of the wall running north-south originally formed the south-eastern corner of a building, of which the east-west return wall is lost. Further to the west loose mud-bricks, some of which are burnt, probably once formed another wall: maybe the south-west corner of the building or an inner division wall. The inside of the building stretched northwards. Remains of a floor can be seen in the section (fig. 5).[16] At some point this building seems to have been abandoned or destroyed according to the accumulation of household debris, which consists of large to medium pieces of pottery, charcoal, ashes and some loose bricks. Later a thick layer of finely laminated silt beds covered the area (fig. 5; pl. II a). Its nature, namely fine layers of silt deposited horizontally, makes it very probable that they

---

[16] The remains of this floor level cannot be traced further west where this layer slopes down considerably. It might be possible that the loose bricks, which once formed a wall, were later inserted into the layer underlying the floor remnants.

a. Old Kingdom Exposure 1, west wall.

b. Old Kingdom Exposure 1, south wall.

Plate I.

a. Old Kingdom Exposure 2

Plate II

were deposited by water. So far the origin of this layer is unclear. Further investigations will be carried out, especially an analysis of the composition of these silt layers in order to draw more precise conclusions. It is possible that extensive rainfall which left standing water or an extremely high Nile flood may have caused them. At present it looks as if the abandonment of the building took place before this layer was deposited. The east wall appears to retain the laminated silt layer. Thus there does not seems to be a connection between the two events.

At some point the building was restored. The lower part of the north-south wall was re-used and built up again. The east-west return wall is set back a few centimetres to the north and built directly on top of the layer with laminated silt-beds (fig. 5; pl. II a). A layer of thick plaster was applied to the joint between these two walls. A few courses of mud bricks bearing traces of plaster were built against the south-west corner of the western wall, which is still preserved today. This mud-brick construction probably functioned as a bench, similar to the benches which can be seen in front of mud-brick houses in modern Egypt.

During the survey in December 2000, samples of pottery were collected in the area around the two Old Kingdom exposures (cf. fig.1). The aim was to find out more about the date of this part of the settlement. The examination of this sample collection will be completed in the next season at Zawiet Sultan in December 2001 and then published separately. Present results suggest that the most chronologically significant types of vessels can be dated possibly to a period between the 5th and 6th Dynasties. The distribution of bread-moulds turned out to be striking. They were scattered in an area within 100 m north and south of the Old Kingdom exposures. No bread-moulds were found in the cemetery area. Although bread-moulds were also placed in burials it seems that here they belong to the settlement debris simply because the tombs are further up the slope and there is no reason to assume that the *sebakhin* would shift large quantities of material from a great distance. The nature of the *sebakh*-digging at the site is characterised by deep pits that have been quarried into the archaeological remains. They were often subsequently back-filled by the sieved-out fragments from another pit close by. Thus pottery would not be removed very far from its original context. This pitted landscape then seems, at least locally, to have been left so that an even weathered surface formed over the top. In the western area of the site, further down the slope, it is noticeable that there are very large dumps of sherds between areas which have been cleared completely down to the bedrock. This indicates that the *sebakh*-diggers removed larger quantities in this part than further up the slope. Maybe it was a second phase of their activities at the site.

In the area between the excavated mastaba tombs and the Old Kingdom exposures many more fragments of mud-brick walls are recognisable within the sherd-heaps, which also can be dated possibly to the Old Kingdom, according to the sherds that are embedded within the

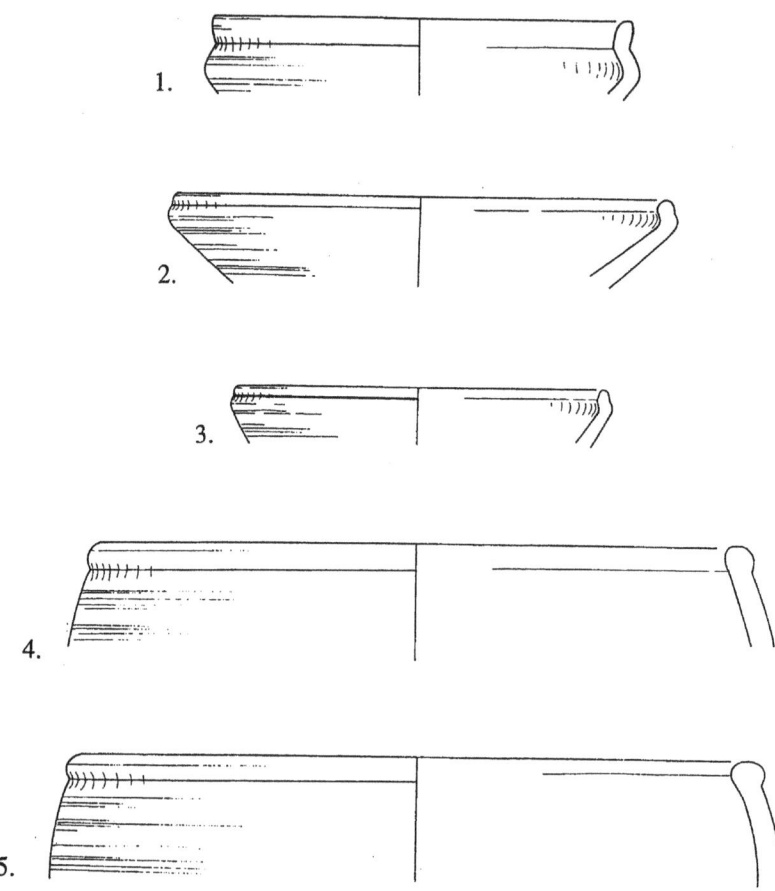

Fig. 6. Old Kingdom pottery from the fill on the southern side of Mastaba I (scale 1:3).

Fine ware with red slip on interior and exterior of vessel surface, burnished, wheelmade, dating to the period between the 5th and 6th Dynasties:

1. Rim of a carinated bowl; fabric: Nile B1.[1] (5th –6th Dynasty).[2]
2. Rim of a carinated bowl; fabric: Nile B1 (6th Dynasty).[3]
3. Rim of a carinated bowl; fabric: Nile B2. (6th Dynasty).[4]
4. Rim of a large, slightly restricted bowl; fabric: Nile B1 (4th-6th Dynasty).[5]
5. Rim of a large, slightly restricted bowl; fabric: Nile B1 (4th-6th Dynasty).[6]

---

[1] The definitions of the fabrics are referring to the "Vienna System", see Nordström and Bourriau 1993, 179-181.
[2] Marchand and Laisney 2000, no.7.
[3] Cf. Kaiser 1969, 61 group XVIII.
[4] Cf. Kaiser 1969, 61 group XVIII.
[5] Cf. Kaiser 1969, 73 group XLV.
[6] Cf. Kaiser 1969, 73 group XLV.

bricks of these walls. No further mud-brick walls were found south of *Old Kingdom exposures 1* and *2*. In this area the bedrock is covered with much less debris and sherds in comparison to the areas further north. There is also a distinctive decrease in Old Kingdom pottery scattered on the surface. Aerial photographs indicate that this region was probably never inhabited. Thus it seems that the southern edge of the Old Kingdom settlement is situated in the area where the Old Kingdom exposures were discovered.

It is also noticeable that the bricks that were used during the Old Kingdom are made of different material compared to those dating to the Graeco-Roman Period: much more organic material in the latter period was used in contrast to mud-bricks from the Old Kingdom, which contain a high percentage of desert marl mixed with fine limestone chippings.

Conclusion about the development of the town

We know nothing of the time of the foundation of the settlement. The small step pyramid that dates to the end of the 3rd / beginning of the 4th Dynasty indicates that at least during that time a settlement might have existed. Today this area is cleared down to the bedrock and it is therefore impossible to find any evidence for Old Kingdom habitation except for a few scattered sherds lying on the surface that can be dated to the 4th – 6th Dynasties.[17] It is quite likely that the earliest part of the town was situated in the vicinity of the pyramid. The area further south, where the Old Kingdom exposures are located, could then be a part of a considerable enlargement of the much smaller settlement. It seems to date to the period between the late 5th and 6th Dynasties. The buildings were built directly on the bedrock and no traces of earlier occupation have been found so far. Such enlargements of settlements dating to the end of the Old Kingdom are known from other sites, for example Dendera[18], where the original, rather small town was enlarged during the latter part of the Old Kingdom. Interestingly so far there are no traces of any occupation or activities dating to the First Intermediate Period or Middle Kingdom at Zawiet Sultan.[19] It seems very probable that the Old Kingdom settlement was abandoned after the 6th Dynasty but it is of course possible that shifts in the course of the Nile have removed evidence of later occupation.[20]

---

[17] This is also confirmed by Kaiser 1961, 35. He found pottery dating to the same periods scattered around the pyramid.
[18] Marchand 2000, 264-77.
[19] Kessler 1980, 211 mentions a Middle Kingdom cemetery that is situated north-east of the pyramid, referring to the publication by Weill 1912, 488. However, Weill does not describe such a cemetery in his report. In another publication by Weill and Jouguet 1934-1937, on page 89 it is mentioned that *"...sous la ville romaine gisaient des cimetières pharaoniques de toutes les époques..."*. Nevertheless this comment does not refer to any actual evidence.
[20] Cf. Butzer 1976, 34.

Acknowledgements

I would like to thank Barry Kemp and Pamela Rose for their kind support and encouragement. The travel and other expenses were awarded by the H.M. Chadwick Fund and The Lady Wallis Budge Fund (Christ's College, Cambridge) for which I am very grateful.

Nadine Moeller
Christ's College
University of Cambridge

Cited Works

Brunner, H.
    1936 *Die Anlagen der ägyptischen Felsgräber bis zum Mittleren Reich. ÄF* 3. Glückstadt: J.J. Augustin.
Brunton, G.
    1937 *Mostagedda and the Tasian Culture. British Museum Expedition to Middle Egypt.First And Second years 1928, 1929*. London: B.Quaritch Ltd. Butzer, K.W.
    1976 *Early Hydraulic Civilization*. Chicago: University of Chicago Press.
Dreyer, G. and W. Kaiser
    1980 'Zu den kleinen Stufenpyramiden Ober- und Mittelägyptens', *MDAIK* 36: 643-59.
Garstang, J.
    1907 *The Burial Customs of Ancient Egypt*. London: Archibald Constable and Co Ltd.
Junker, H.
    1943 *Giza VI. Die Mastabas des Nefer, Kedfl, Kahjef und die westlich anschließenden Grabanlagen*. Wien: Holder-Pichler-Tempsky.
Kaiser, W.
    1961 'Bericht über eine archäologisch-geologische Felduntersuchung in Ober-und Mittelägypten', *MDAIK* 17: 1-68.
Kemp, B.J.
    1977 'The early development of towns in Egypt', *Antiquity* 51: 185-200.
Kessler, D.
    1981 *Historische Topographie der Region zwischen Mallawi und Samalut. TAVO Beih. 19*. Wiesbaden: Dr. Ludwig Reichert Verlag.
Lepsius, K.R.
    1904 *Denkmaeler aus Aegypten und Aethiopien*. Text II. Leipzig: J.C.Hinrichs'sche Buchhandlung.
Mace, A.C.
    1909 *The Early Dynastic Cemeteries of Naga-ed-Dêr. Part III*. Leipzig: J.C.Hinrichs.
Marchand, S. and D. Laisney.
    2000 'Le survey de Dendera (1996-1997)', *Cahiers de la Céramique Égyptienne* 6: 246-77.
Nordström, H.-Å. and J. Bourriau.
    1993 'Ceramic Technology: Clays and Fabrics', in: D. Arnold and J. Bourriau (eds.). *An*

Introduction to Ancient Egyptian Pottery. Mainz: Phillip von Zabern.

Osing, J.
1992 *Das Grab des Nefersecheru in Zawyet Sultan.* AV 88. Mainz: Phillip von Zabern.

Quibell, J.E.
1898 *El Kab*. British School of Archaeology in Egypt and Egyptian Research Account 1897. Vol. 3. London: B.Quaritch Ltd.

Reisner, G.A.
1932 A Provincial Cemetery of the Pyramid Age. Naga-ed-Dêr. Part III. Berkeley (CA): University of California Press.

1936 *The Development of the Egyptian Tomb down to the Accession of Cheops*. Cambridge: Harvard University Press.

Seidlmayer, S.J.
1990 *Gräberfelder aus dem Übergang vom Alten zum Mittleren Reich*. SAGA 1. Heidelberg: Heidelberger Orientverlag.

Spencer, A.J.
1993 *Excavations at El-Ashmunein III. The Town*. London: British Museum Press.

Weill, R.
1912 'Fouilles a Tounah et a Zaouiét El-Maietin (Moyenne Égypte)', *CRAIBL*: 484-90.

Weill, R. and P. Jouguet
1934-1937 'Horus-Apollon au Kôm el-Ahmar de Zwaiet el-Maietin', *MIFAO* 67: 81-104.

EGYPT AND MYCENAEAN GREECE: A MYCENAEAN PERSPECTIVE

Georgina Muskett

Both archaeological and documentary evidence suggests intense contact between the various areas surrounding the Eastern Mediterranean in the 15th to the 13th centuries BC.[1] In this paper, I shall be noting, firstly, evidence for the awareness of Mycenaeans in Egypt and vice versa. Secondly, I intend to focus on the main features of the presentation in life of the Mycenaean elite and, where surviving contexts permit, make comparisons with analogous representations in Egypt. Finally, I shall be discussing certain aspects of Egyptian art which are not present on the Greek mainland, and vice versa, and suggest reasons for these differences.

In Egypt, awareness of Mycenaean Greece is indicated in several contexts. Mycenaean pottery has been found at a range of sites in Egypt, from the reigns of several rulers, suggesting the frequent exchange of commodities from the Mycenaean world to Egypt.[2] No LHI pottery has been found to date in Egypt,[3] although LHIIA material has been found at Sakkara and Thebes, and LHIIB at Kahun.[4] Most of the ceramic material at el-Amarna is LHIIIA2, although LHIIIB pottery is quite rare in Egypt.[5]

There is documentary evidence of knowledge of the Aegean region in the so-called "Aegean List", inscribed on a statue base from the mortuary temple of Amenhotep III at Kom el-Hetan, on the west bank at Thebes.[6] The Aegean List is a series of place names or toponyms, referring to areas or regions seemingly connected with Egypt during the reign of Amenhotep III,[7] given in the form of hieroglyphs within an oval with projections, above the figure of a bound prisoner, a normal New Kingdom iconographic convention for indicating a foreigner.[8] The list of toponyms includes Mycenae, together with a reference to Tanaja, possibly vocalized as a version of *Danaoi*, which could refer to the Mycenaeans.[9]

There are no definite depictions of Mycenaeans among the individuals named as "Keftiu" in Egyptian tomb paintings,[10] although I believe that the person identified as "Keftiu" in the Memphite tomb of Horemheb could be Mycenaean,[11] due to the late date of the tomb. In addition, there is the possible representation of Mycenaean[12] soldiers[13] on fragments of painted papyrus from el-Amarna.[14] The papyrus was found in House R43.2, the so-called "House of the King's Statue", now identified as a chapel,[15] in association with a Mycenaean stirrup jar, dated to LHIIIA2 late.[16] It has been estimated that the original design showed approximately fifteen warriors, possibly running to assist a captured Egyptian soldier. The group of warriors wear Egyptian-style kilts, although the pale yellow helmets, worn by two soldiers, may be made from boar's tusks,[17] characteristic of Mycenaean soldiers, and two wear ox-hide tunics, similar to examples depicted on Mycenaean Pictorial Style pottery.[18] Both the scene, the only known example of a pictorial papyrus to show a battle,[19] and elements of the composition, appear unusual, not least the Egyptian being killed by an enemy[20] and the favourable representation of foreigners.

On the Greek mainland, particularly at Mycenae, artifacts originating in Egypt, the majority from the 18th and 19th Dynasties, are found in a range of contexts throughout the Late Bronze Age.[21] The artifacts found in LHIIIA1-B2 contexts comprise easily portable items such as vases of various materials, scarabs, figurines and other small items made of faience and steatite; that is, the type of items one would expect to be part of exchange networks in the Eastern Mediterranean at this time. Particularly interesting examples have been found at Prosymna; a

---

[1] Morgan (1988, 172) notes that the only iconographic evidence of interrelations in the Eastern Mediterranean are in Egyptian tombs, showing foreigners bringing goods to Egypt; for discussion and illustration of these representations, see Wachsmann 1987.
[2] Evidence up to 1993 given by Hankey 1993, 112.
[3] Of the list of vases found in Egypt, dated by Wace and Blegen (1939, 145-6) to LHI and II, no item is definitely LHI.
[4] Mountjoy 1993, 167-9.
[5] Mountjoy 1993, 174.
[6] The statue base inscribed with the Aegean List (Cline 1987, 2, figs.1-2) is no longer either intact, or *in situ*, apparently accidentally destroyed some time after 1975 (Schofield and Parkinson 1994, 158; Cline 1998, 236-7).
[7] Various opinions regarding the date of compilation of the Aegean List are summarised, with full bibliography, by Cline 1987, 4.
[8] Cline 1987, 5.
[9] The full list of 17 names, with a review of suggested interpretations, in Cline 1987, 26-30, Table 2.

---

[10] Wachsmann (1987, 109-110) does not believe that Mycenaeans are depicted in Theban tombs.
[11] The decoration of the south wall is unfinished, with no surviving text, and shows a group of individuals, identified via dress and hairstyles, from Libya, Western Asia, Nubia and the Aegean. Although non-Egyptians are depicted elsewhere in the tomb, this is the only representation of someone who can be identified as Aegean (Martin 1991, 48, fig.14.)
[12] Schofield and Parkinson 1994, 170; *contra* Rehak (1999, 230, n.29) who observes they wear Egyptian-style kilts.
[13] Schofield and Parkinson (1994, 169) and Cline (1995b, 270-1) believe they are mercenaries.
[14] Cline 1994: 36, 108, no.A.6; Schofield and Parkinson 1994; 1995; Parkinson and Schofield 1995; 1997.
[15] Parkinson and Schofield 1997, 401.
[16] Hankey 1995, 116, no.3.
[17] Schofield and Parkinson 1994, 166, Parkinson and Schofield 1997, 403. Rehak (1999, 230) observes that boars' tusk helmets may have been exchanged between the Greek mainland and other societies in the Eastern Mediterranean, including Egypt. Possible evidence of such helmets in Egypt in Pusch 1985, 254 (worked boar's tusk from Qantir, in a context from the reign of Ramesses II).
[18] Schofield and Parkinson 1994, 167.
[19] Schofield and Parkinson 1994, 160.
[20] Schofield and Parkinson (1994, 162) note an absence of visual parallels for an Egyptian killed by an enemy.
[21] Cline 1994, Table 64.

small carnelian hippopotamus[22] and a steatite scarab, the latter's inscription suggesting it dates from the 18th Dynasty.[23]

Fig. 1. Male figure, possibly wearing a boar's tusk helmet and oxhide tunic, from a painted papyrus found at el-Amarna. Not to scale.
After Parkinson and Schofild 1997.

Possibly different in nature are a small number of items with inscriptions suggesting associations with rulers of the 18th Dynasty. The earliest inscriptions are on two fragmentary figurines, in the form of a monkey, made of faience, from Mycenae[24] and Tiryns[25] each with a cartouche containing Amenhotep II's prenomen on its right arm. There is more extensive epigraphic evidence referring to Amenhotep III and Queen Tiy. Artefacts from Mycenae include a faience vase with a cartouche of Amenhotep III[26] and two faience scarabs, inscribed with the name of Queen Tiy.[27] Such objects are found at other sites, however; a faience scarab, inscribed with the name of Amenhotep III, was found in a chamber tomb at Ayios Elias in Aetolia.[28]

The most intriguing objects are fragmentary plaques, made of white faience, possibly originally blue- or green-glazed,[29] from various contexts at Mycenae, inscribed with Egyptian hieroglyphs in black on both sides. They are a unique find; there are no plaques of this type anywhere else outside Egypt.[30] Cline has identified eleven fragments, which he believes were originally from six to nine plaques, all from LHIIIB contexts,[31] with the most extensive inscription on seven fragments from the acropolis at Mycenae.[32]

The exact significance of the faience plaques has raised widely differing views. Cline observes that virtually all the plaques, together with the majority of Amenhotep III or Queen Tiy inscribed objects, are found in either votive contexts, or associated with figurines, suggesting that, at least in Mycenae, there was awareness of the fact that, in Egypt, similar plaques were used in a religious context, under statues, temples and other buildings.[33] In addition, both Hankey[34] and Cline[35] suggest the plaques were associated with an official visit by Egyptians to Mycenae late in the reign of Amenhotep III.[36]

However, Lilyquist observes that exact parallels between the plaques from Mycenae and actual Egyptian objects are absent, and, therefore, the plaques may have been of

---

[22] National Museum, Athens 6427; Cline 1993, 226.
[23] National Museum, Athens 8450; Cline 1993, 226.
[24] Seated monkey, unknown context. National Museum, Athens 4573. Extant H.3.5cm, extant W.1.5cm, Th. of body 1.3cm. Lambrou-Phillipson 1990, 64, 343, no. 437; Cline 1991, 30-3, pl.Ia-d; 1994, 132, no.5, fig.19.
[25] Female monkey holding an infant against her stomach. Tiryns Inv.no.LXI 36/88a 12 46. LHIIIA context. Extant H.3.8cm, extant W.1.8cm, Th. of body 1.3cm. Cline 1991, 34-5, pl.IIa-c; 1994, 132, no.6, fig.20.
[26] Chamber Tomb 49. National Museum, Athens 2491; Cline 1994, 216, no.734, pl.3.10.

[27] a)Room 19, Cult Centre. Mycenae Exc.No. 68-1521. L.1.3, W.1.0. Cline 1987, 10, n.41; 1994, 146, no.119; 1995a, 99, no.17; Lambrou-Phillipson 1990, no.439, pl.53. a) Room Γ, "Tsountas' House." National Museum, Athens 2530. L.1.7, W.1.3. Cline 1987, 10, n.41; 1994, 146, no.120; 1995a, 99, no.18; Lambrou-Phillipson 1990, no.438, pl.53.
[28] Patras Museum 213. L.1.6, W.1.3. Cline 1987, 23; 1994, 146, no.123; Lambrou-Phillipson 1990, no.256, pl.52.
[29] Although note the comments of Andreopoulou-Mangou (1988, 18) that in contrast to the bright blue or blue-green glaze which is characteristic of Egyptian faience, the glaze of Aegean faience tends to be "whitish", that is, various shades of light grey or brown and, accordingly, the present colour of the plaques could reflect their original colour (cf. Lilyquist 1999, 305-6).
[30] Cline 1990, 201-2.
[31] Cline 1990, 202.
[32] National Museum, Athens 2566, 1-5, 2718 and 12582. Cline 1990, 201; 1994, 143, no.98; Lambrou-Phillipson 1990, 64, nos. 440-6, pl.63. Also two non-joining fragments from the Cult Centre, the larger inscribed on both sides with the prenomen of Amenhotep III, probably part of the same plaque (National Museum, Athens 68-100 and 69-126. L.9.7, W.11.2, Th.1.25-1.55 and National Museum, Athens 69-126, L.5, W.4, Th.1.3. Taylour 1969, 94-5; Cline 1990, 200-1, pls.1-2, figs.1-2; 1994, 143, no.97; Lambrou-Phillipson 1990, 64, no. 448, pl.64) and a further two fragments from the acropolis (Formerly Nafplion Museum 13-887 and 13-888, destined for the new museum at Mycenae); L.7.3, W.7.5 and L.6.3cm, W.6.3cm; Cline 1990, 201; 1994, 143, no.96; Lambrou-Phillipson 1990, 64, no.447, pl.64).
[33] Cline, 1990, 208.
[34] Hankey 1981, 45-6.
[35] Cline 1987, 23; 1994, 39-41.
[36] Cline further suggests the Aegean List is an itinerary of this visit, with a possible correlation between the places listed and major centres, which have also produced Amenhotep III or Queen Tiyi inscribed objects (Cline 1987; 1994, 38-42; 1995a, 94-5; 1998, 245-6).

barely more significance than the small Egyptian items, such as the scarabs referred to above.[37] Not only is the fabric of the core of the plaques darker than is normally the case with high-quality faience from the reign of Amenhotep III,[38] but analysis indicates that one of the plaques[39] contains lead from the Lavrion region of Attica,[40] strongly suggesting it was made on the Greek mainland.[41] This, I believe, denotes a desire for display incorporating Egyptian, or Egyptianising, features, in a similar manner to the situation in the Early Mycenaean period, which saw the imitation of Minoan items, manifest in both the use of Minoan iconography and the "pseudo-Minoan" class of pottery; that is, vessels which are such close copies of Minoan vases they have been considered imports when found on the Greek mainland.[42] The presence of Egyptian-style faience plaques at Mycenae may be explained by a similar analogy; the plaques may have been the work of an Egyptian resident at, or visiting, Mycenae, [43]or of a Mycenaean aware of Egyptian artefacts or techniques.[44]

Turning now to the main features of the presentation of the elite in domestic contexts in Mycenaean Greece, the extant remains of the decoration of the palace at Pylos[45] suggest the depiction of rituals required to maintain the security of the state, whereas the ruling elite at Mycenae[46] chose to depict warfare, plausibly to signal their expertise in battle and deter potential rivals. In Egypt, the surviving decoration of New Kingdom palaces includes scenes with no counterpart in Mycenaean Greece, despite a predominance of warlike themes in the latter society. Amenhotep III was shown throughout the palace at Malkata[47] keeping order within his kingdom by overcoming foreign enemies, including representations on stone columns and doorjambs. At Malkata, the king even appeared to walk on and sit above his enemies, suggested by figures of bound captives painted on the floor and treads of the steps of a dais, apparently for a throne.[48] Similar depictions of bound captives are found in the "North Harim" at the Great Palace at Amarna, where large floor paintings were connected by a painted pathway of Asiatic and Nubian captives, forming a continuous line of prisoners.[49] In addition, the sides of raised platforms at the "King's House in Amarna"[50] and at 19th Dynasty royal palaces at Memphis and Qantir were painted with similar images.[51] This type of decoration is illustrated by a painting in the tomb chapel of Anen at Thebes, depicting Amenhotep III and Queen Tiy seated on a throne dais at Malkata. The dais is decorated with a row of kneeling, bound captives, identified as non-Egyptian by their dress and hairstyles. The side panel of the king's throne shows his image as a sphinx, trampling foreign enemies, and two prostrate foreigners are depicted on his footstool.[52]

The other scant remains of the decorative schemes of Egyptian palaces[53] have produced no evidence of scenes which may have influenced Mycenaean wall painting. Although Mycenaean "procession frescoes" are possibly derived initially from Egypt via Crete,[54] Mycenaean examples are found overwhelmingly in domestic and cult contexts rather than funerary contexts,[55] a sharp contrast to Egypt. Equally, the items carried in Mycenaean "procession frescoes" appear cult offerings, rather than items of "tribute" or even gift exchange. The surviving wall paintings from the palace at Malkata are extremely fragmentary, with nothing suggesting the depiction of a procession.[56]

When considering the influence of Egypt on Early Mycenaean art, evidence from the shaft graves at Mycenae suggests it was minimal,[57] despite attempts to suggest the contrary by Meurer,[58] Persson,[59] Marinatos[60]

---

[37] Lilyquist 1999, 303-5; cf. Wachsmann 1987,113, who believes that they were merely exotic *objets d'art*, which arrived on the Greek mainland as a result of indirect trade. Despite Cline's (1998, 158) observation that the plaques are more substantial in size than scarabs, I would comment that the extant fragments suggest they were fairly small and, if not made at Mycenae, would have caused no difficulties in transportation.
[38] Lilyquist 1999, 304.
[39] National Museum, Athens 68-1000, the larger fragment from the Cult Centre at Mycenae.
[40] According to Lilyquist and Brill (1993, 61, n.10), it is "Lavrion or Lavrion-like lead".
[41] Lilyquist 1999, 306.
[42] Mountjoy 1999, 21.
[43] Lilyquist (1999, 304) notes that the plaques "show good Egyptian palaeography".
[44] cf. Cline 1990, 210; Lilyquist 1999, 306.
[45] Illustrated by Lang 1969.
[46] Illustrated by Rodenwaldt 1921, 21-45, Beilagen I-IV and colour plate; Lamb 1921-3.
[47] Interpreted by Kemp and Weatherhead (2000, 520) as a "seasonal retret", possibly in use during the king's first two jubilee festivals.
[48] Robins 1997, 136; Smith 1981, 286; Weatherhead 1992, 192.

[49] Weatherhead 1992, 179, 187, figs. 1, 4 and 5; Kemp and Weatherhead 2000, 508, figs.1, 3. Kemp and Weatherhead (2000, 508) observe similarities to a design carved into alabaster paving in another area of the Great Palace.
[50] Weatherhead 1995, 98-102, pl.VII,1, figs.3-4.
[51] Weatherhead 1992, 192; 1995, 103.
[52] Robins 1997, 136, fig.155; Wachsmann 1987, pl.XLVIII. The detail of the individual labelled as "Keftiu" is shown by Wachsmann 1987, pl. LA, although he observes that the figure is composed of Syrian and Hittite as well as Aegean elements (Wachsmann 1987, 40).
[53] Summarised in Smith 1981, 281, 286, 295 and Kemp and Weatherhead 2000. Also note fragments from Site K, a plaster dump at the periphery of the palatial area at Malkata, believed to have been from the First Jubilee structure of Amenhotep III, demolished shortly after construction. Although the style of the paintings was predominantly Egyptian in character, a few elements, such as the imitation of marbling, inclusion of rosettes, and the use of rocky landscape may have been borrowed from the Aegean repertoire (Nicolakaki-Kentrou 2000). My thanks to Ian Buckley for drawing my attention to this reference.
[54] Immerwahr 1990, 89-90.
[55] Immerwahr 1990, Th.No.7 is a rare exception.
[56] Although note a life-size representation of a woman wearing a tall headdress, from the second audience hall of the king's palace (Peterson 1981, 156, ill.145; Smith 1981, fig.59).
[57] cf. Vermeule 1975, 18, "there is nothing truly Egyptian in the Shaft Graves". Also note Touchais' (1999, 203-5) remarks refuting suggestions of close links between mainland Greece and Egypt in this period.
[58] Meurer 1912, pl.12, reconstructed one of the female burials in Grave III in an anthropoid coffin, decorated with gold ornaments found in the tomb.

and Mylonas.[61] In the case of the few artifacts which appear Egyptian in origin, such as a vessel made from pale yellow faience[62] and an alabaster jar, of a type known from 18th Dynasty Egypt, modified by being inverted, and by having the additions of a spout, and gold leaf around the rim, handles and foot,[63] I believe they were probably imported to the Greek mainland via Crete.

In LHIIIA-B, however, if one accepts a certain level of contact between Egypt and Mycenaean Greece, it would surely be plausible that this connection would be reflected in artistic production. Consideration of the surviving material from various centres on the Greek mainland – even Mycenae, where the concentration of Egyptian material is greatest – suggests, I believe, that the ruling elite were unwilling to accept Egyptian iconography, and almost totally rejected large-scale sculpture, a major feature of Egyptian art in this period.

To attempt an explanation for this phenomenon, I believe it is essential to differentiate between, firstly, items originating in Egypt and, secondly, the extent to which contact with Egypt influenced artistic production and, consequently, the presentation of the elite on the Greek mainland. In the case of the former, I consider that caution should be exercised in attaching too much significance to discoveries of ceramics; this merely suggests that the societies involved were members of the same trading and exchange networks, and, in addition, the amounts involved were comparatively small; the same comments apply to other portable items, plausibly mere *objets d'art*, coveted because of their exotic provenance. Furthermore, it is important not to assume that each of the sites with iconographic links were in direct contact with each other.[64] With regard to the second aspect, the incomplete survival of the archaeological record on the Greek mainland and Egypt means a comprehensive assessment is impossible. However, it appears there were not only differences in the contexts considered suitable for elite display, but also certain conventions of iconography applied in both societies, which appeared unaffected by the links between them.

Although iconographic transfer clearly took place, with Mycenaean and Egyptian artists making use of forms and motifs used by external societies, they were employed as lesser elements only, and major artistic conventions were unaffected.[65] Indeed, although motifs borrowed from other artistic traditions exerted an influence in Mycenaean art, their importance was less than they had been during the transition from the Middle to Late Bronze Age.[66] I believe that it is unwise to over-state similarities in the iconography of artifacts from areas with different artistic traditions. For example, although there are apparent similarities in terms of theme in the case of LHIIIC Pictorial Style sherds from central Greece showing warships[67] and contemporary Egyptian sculpted reliefs, one must consider whether this is due to iconographic transfer, or merely that artists in both societies were depicting scenes reflecting historical reality of that period.[68] I would also urge caution in assuming that iconographic elements found in different societies carry the same meaning and connotations irrespective of wherever they are found.[69]

Turning to the media used for representational art, it is apparent that large-scale sculpture was incorporated into specific Egyptian contexts, which did not exist in Mycenaean Greece. Furthermore, with the exception of the carved relief which decorates the "Lion Gate" at Mycenae and slabs of gypsum from the Treasury of Atreus, carved with images of bulls,[70] that medium- and large-scale sculpture is totally absent from LHIIIA-B Greece, and was rejected by the ruling elite as a suitable medium through which to express their identity. This absence cannot be explained by unfamiliarity with handling masonry, as this is evident in the construction of massive fortification walls and tholos tombs.

The same is true regarding the subjects depicted by Mycenaean artists. The evidence suggests a complete lack of representations of anyone who can be identified with any certainty as a ruler or leader at any of the Mycenaean palatial sites, a remarkable contrast with Egypt. In addition, despite an apparent preference for the Mycenaean elite to incorporate scenes of warfare in the decoration of the palaces, there are marked differences from the way in which this type of iconography is used in Egypt. In Egyptian battle scenes showing the Pharaoh, there is only one winner – the Egyptian ruler and his armies – and the sense of superiority is always emphasized. By contrast, representations of battle scenes

---

[59] Persson 1942, 179-81, regarding a wooden box from Grave V, with attachments in the form of dogs (Karo 1930-3, 144, no.812, pl.CXLV), although there is nothing about the item which suggests Egyptian origins, cf. Hooker 1967, 278; Hood 1978, 115.

[60] Marinatos 1951 regarding a silver pin with gold head, from Grave III, in the form of a woman in Minoan-style costume, surrounded by papyrus flowers (Karo 1930-3, no.75, pl.XXX), suggesting it was a Cretan artist's attempt to render an Egyptian allegory. There is, however, no evidence that Egyptian motifs ever had more than a decorative meaning in Crete (cf. Hooker 1967, 278).

[61] Mylonas (1969) suggested that the well-preserved body in Grave V was Egyptian, on the basis of what he believed was "embalming" and the nature of certain offerings.

[62] From Grave II. Karo 1930-3, no.223, pl.CLXX; Cline 1995a, 104, no.70.

[63] Grave V. Karo 1930-3, no.829, pl.CXXXVII; Cline 1995a, 102, no.51. cf. the similar modification of an Egyptian alabaster jar from Chamber Tomb 68, Mycenae (Cline 1995a, 102, no.54).

[64] Morgan 1988, 171.

[65] cf. Smith 1981, 222.

[66] Crowley 1991, 226.

[67] Dakoronia 1990,122, figs.1-3.

[68] Hiller 1999, 327.

[69] cf. Doumas 1992, 29, who observes that iconographic elements in the Thera wall paintings are found in the artistic traditions of other societies surrounding the eastern Mediterranean, but should be interpreted as evidence of the close connections between the various areas, and may have been used to "express different ideas or to serve different ends in each case."

[70] British Museum Catalogue of Sculpture nos.A56 and A57. Younger (1995, 343, n.61) believes they were possibly Minoan imports.

from Mycenaean Greece do not always make it clear who is the victor. This can be seen in a battle scene from the palace at Pylos,[71] where one group of fighters wearing kilts, greaves and boars' tusk helmets – presumably the Pylian elite – confront bare-legged opponents, possibly wearing white animal skins.[72] Although one white-clad figure has been stabbed, and another lies prostrate, one of the fighters wearing a boars' tusk helmet also appears dead or wounded.

It is surely correct that the scenes from the palace at Mycenae, showing preparations for battle and the battle itself,[73] suggest not only the concerns of the ruling elite, but are also a statement of power.[74] However, the focus is exclusively on the power of the Mycenaean elite, with no reference to the subjection of their opponents, either real or potential. This is a strong contrast to Egypt, where, as discussed above, an iconographic convention during the New Kingdom to indicate a foreigner was the use of hieroglyphs within an oval, above the figure of a captive prisoner. Typical examples of an Egyptian battle scene are found on the long sides of a wooden chest from the tomb of Tutankhamun. The composition is dominated by the large figure of the king in his chariot, and whereas the Egyptian troops appear very ordered and in control, the enemies - Nubians on one side, Syrians on the other - are in disarray. Egyptian domination is emphasized by the scenes on the end panels of the chest, in which Tutankhamun is shown as a sphinx trampling Egypt's northern and southern enemies.[75]

Although hunting scenes are known from both the Mycenaean[76] and Egyptian artistic repertoire, the elements of the composition are very different in the two societies. In marked contrast to surviving depictions of hunting from the Greek mainland from LHIIIA-B,[77] the focus of elite hunting scenes in Egypt is invariably the king. Typical Egyptian images appear on the central panels of a bow-case and on a fan from the tomb of Tutankhamun. The bow-case shows the king in his chariot, firing his bow, accompanied by dogs.[78] The fan is decorated with scenes of the king shooting at ostriches, and returning from the hunt, accompanied by attendants carrying the birds.[79] The lid of the wooden chest from this tomb, discussed above, was painted with hunting scenes showing the dominant figure of the king, accompanied by a retinue of attendants, on a smaller scale.[80]

It can be seen, therefore, that, as in the Early Mycenaean period, the acquisition of items perceived as exotic in terms of media or iconography was still considered desirable, but the extent to which these items influenced Mycenaean artistic production is much less marked than the enormous effects of contacts with Minoan Crete, visible in all aspects of Early Mycenaean arts for the elite. By LHIIIA-B, the period when the majority of items from Egypt reached the Greek mainland, the Mycenaean elite had apparently formulated their own distinctive iconographic repertoire, albeit making full use of materials not native to the Greek mainland, such as ivory. Although some items appeared in mainland Greece which are plausibly mere *objets d'art*, coveted because of their exotic provenance, together with inscribed items, some of which may be locally-made pastiches of true Egyptian items, the main cornerstone of Egyptian art – large-scale sculpture, either relief or free-standing – is virtually absent. I believe the reason for this absence is not merely differences of context – an obvious example being the vast differences between the setting for cult activities in Egypt and on the Greek mainland – but also the remarkable disparity between the presentation of the ruler in these societies. Indeed, there is no representation from the Greek mainland identified with any degree of certainty as a ruler. The Mycenaeans were not iconoclasts; the surviving evidence includes many representations of the human face and form from a wide range of contexts. The nature of society was such that an individual was presented as a member of a ruling elite rather than as an individual ruler, although I believe that the attested interconnections suggest the Mycenaeans were aware of the conventions of ruler iconography.[81] Indeed, certain iconographic conventions were apparently unacceptable in Mycenaean Greece. Although the presentation of elite males traditionally included animal iconography,[82] and association with wild boar by using its tusks in helmets[83] the concept of representing the ruler as a sphinx, that is, with the body of a lion, was seemingly rejected in Mycenaean Greece, although the Near Eastern form of winged sphinx was a popular motif on the Greek mainland in this period.[84]

I would conclude, therefore, that even if the nature of the relationship between mainland Greece and and Egypt was more than participants in the same exchange networks – and, indeed, portable items such as statuettes and scarabs would not necessarily require the presence of foreigners on the Greek mainland and vice versa in the case of Mycenaean ceramics in Egypt – and there were diplomatic, even military links between Egypt and

---

[71] Lang 1969,no.22 H 64, pls.16, 117, A, M and no.25 H 64, pls.19, N; Immerwahr 1990, Py.No.10, pl.66.
[72] Lang 1969, 71.
[73] Rodenwaldt 1921, 21-45, Beilagen I-IV, colour plate.
[74] cf. similar comments by Peterson 1981, 24.
[75] Smith 1965, 167; Robins 1997, fig.189.
[76] For discussion of this topic, see Immerwahr 1990, 129-33.
[77] e.g. Immerwahr 1990, Or.No.3, Ti.No.6.
[78] Carter 1954, 190-1.
[79] Carter 1954, 90-1; Smith 1965, 167; Robins 1997, fig.189.
[80] Carter 1954, 46-7.

[81] cf. Rehak 1995, 96, n.9. It is possible that visitors from the Aegean to Egypt would have seen some painted reliefs in Egyptian tombs, especially in the hall giving access to the chapel for ritual offerings, which would have been permanently open. In addition, representations in public areas of Egyptian palaces would have been visible (Peterson 1981, 156; Smith 1965, 134).
[82] e.g. gold seal showing a man-lion duel, from Shaft Grave III, Mycenae; National Museum, Athens 33.
[83] Morgan 1988: 112.
[84] Many examples in a variety of media, e.g. ivory pyxis from Chamber Tomb 1, Megalo Kastelli, Thebes Archaeological Museum 2828; gold ring, Chamber Tomb 91, Mycenae, National Museum, Athens 3182.

Greece in LHIIIA-B, this was barely reflected in the artistic production of the latter. I believe that this was almost certainly due to the massive differences between the presentation of the ruler in Egypt and Mycenaean Greece and, more generally, the commemorative and, therefore, individualized, character of Egyptian art compared to the generic nature of Mycenaean art.

Acknowledgements

I wish to acknowledge the support of Professor Christopher Mee, my research supervisor, who was kind enough to read this article in draft form, and made many useful suggestions. In addition, as noted in the text, Ian Buckley provided an extremely helpful reference. The research for this article was undertaken while I was the holder of a postgraduate studentship awarded by the Arts and Humanities Research Board.

Cited works

Andreopoulou-Mangou, E.
    1988 'Chemical analysis of faience objects in the National Archaeological Museum', in R.E. Jones and H.W. Catling (eds.), *New Aspects of Archaeological Science in Greece*. Occasional Paper 3 of the Fitch Laboratory. Athens: 15-18.

Carter, H.
    1954. *The Tomb of Tutankhamen*. London: Sphere.

Cline, E.
    1987 'Amenhotep III and the Aegean. A reassessment of Egypto-Aegean relations in the 14th century BC', *Orientalia* 56: 1-36.
    1990 An unpublished Amenhotep III faience plaque from Mycenae', *JAOS* 110: 200-12.
    1991 'Monkey business in the Bronze Age Aegean: the Amenhotep II faience figurines at Mycenae and Tiryns', *Annual of the British School at Athens* 86: 29-42.
    1994 *Sailing the Wine-Dark Sea: International Trade and the Late Bronze Age Aegean*. British Archaeological Reports International Series 591. Oxford.
    1995a 'Egyptian and Near Eastern Imports in Late Bronze Age Mycenae', in W.V. Davies and L. Schofield (eds.), *Egypt, the Aegean and the Levant: Interconnections in the Second Millennium BC*. London: British Museum Press: 91-115.
    1995b 'Tinker, tailor, soldier, sailor: Minoans and Mycenaeans abroad', in R. Laffineur and W-D Niemeier (eds.), *Politeia: Society and state in the Aegean Bronze Age*. Aegaeum 12: Liège: 265-87.
    1998 'Amenhotep III, the Aegean, and Anatolia', in D. O'Connor and E. H. Cline (eds.), *Amenhotep III: perspectives on his reign*. Ann Arbor, Michigan: 236-50.

Crowley, J.L.
    1991 'Patterns in the sea: insight into the artistic vision of the Aegeans', in R. Laffineur and L. Basch (eds.), *Thalassa: l'Égée Préhistorique et la Mer*. Aegaeum 7. Liège: 219-30.

Dakoronia, F.
    1990 'War-ships on sherds of LHIIIC kraters from Kynos?', in H. Tzalas (ed.), *Tropis II: 2nd international symposium on ship construction in antiquity*. Athens: Hellenic Institute for the Preservation of Nautical Tradition: 117-22.

Doumas, C.
    1992 *The Wall Paintings of Thera*. Athens: Thera Foundation.

Hankey, V.
    1981 'The Aegean interest in el-Amarna', *Journal of Mediterranean Anthropology and Archaeology* 1: 28-49.
    1993 'Pottery as evidence for trade: Egypt', in C. Zerner (ed.), *Wace and Blegen: Pottery as Evidence for Trade in the Aegean Bronze Age 1939-1987*. Amsterdam: Gleben: 109-16.
    1995 'Stirrup jars at el-Amarna', in W.V. Davies and L. Schofield (eds.), *Egypt, the Aegean and the Levant: Interconnections in the Second Millennium BC*. London: British Museum Press: 116-24.

Hiller, S.
    1999 'Scenes of warfare and combat in the arts of Aegean Late Bronze Age. Reflections on typology and development', in R. Laffineur (ed.), *Polemos: Le contexte guerrier en Égée a l'Âge du Bronze*. Aegaeum 19. Liège: 319-330.

Hood, M.S.F.
    1978 *The Arts in Prehistoric Greece*. London: Penguin.

Hooker, J.T.
    1967 'The Mycenae Siege Rhyton and the question of Egyptian influence' *AJA* 71: 269-81.

Immerwahr, S.A.
    1990 *Aegean Painting in the Bronze Age*. University Park (Pa.): Pennsylvania State University Press.

Karo, G.
    1930-33 *Die Schachtgräber von Mykenai*. Munich: F. Bruckmann.

Kemp, B. and F. Weatherhead.
    2000 'Palace decoration at Tell el-Amarna', in S. Sherratt (ed.), *The Wall Paintings of Thera. Proceedings of the First International Symposium*, I. Athens: Thera Foundation: 491-523.

Lambrou-Phillipson, C.
    1990 *Hellenorientalia. The Near Eastern Presence in the Bronze Age Aegean, ca.3000-1100 B.C.*

Lamb, W.
(Studies in Mediterranean Archaeology Pocket-Book 95. Göteborg.
1921-3 'Excavations at Mycenae: Palace Frescoes'. *Annual of the British School at Athens* 25: 249-255.

Lang, M.L.
1969 *The Palace of Nestor at Pylos in Western Messenia, Vol. II: The Frescoes.* Princeton (NJ): Princeton University Press.

Lilyquist, C.
1999 'On the Amenhotep III inscribed faience fragments from Mycenae', *JAOS* 119 (2): 303-8.

Lilyquist, C. and R.H. Brill
1993 *Studies in Early Egyptian Glass.* New York: Metropolitan Museum of Art.

Marinatos, S.
1951 '"Numerous years of joyful life" from Mycenae', *Annual of the British School at Athens* 46: 102-16.

Martin, G.T.
1991 *The Hidden Tombs of Memphis. New Discoveries from the Time of Tutankhamun and Ramesses the Great.* London: Thames and Hudson.

Meurer, M
1912. 'Der Goldschmuch der mykenischen Schachtgräber', *Jahrbuch des deutschen archäologischen Instituts* 27: 208-27.

Morgan, L.
1988 *The Miniature Wall Paintings of Thera: A Study in Aegean Culture and Iconography.* Cambridge: Cambridge University Press.

Mountjoy, P.A.
1993 *Mycenaean Pottery: an Introduction.* Oxford University Committee for Archaeology, Monograph No. 36.Oxford.

Mountjoy, P.A.
1999 *Regional Mycenaean Decorated Pottery.* Rahden: M. Leidorf.

Mylonas, G.E.
1969 "Ὁ πέμπτος λακκοειδής τάφος τοῦ κύκλου Α τῶν Μυκηνῶν", Ἀρχαιολογική Ἐφημερίς: 125-42.

Nicolakaki-Kentrou, M.
2000 'Malkata, Site K: the Aegean-related motifs in the painted decoration of a demolished building of Amenhotep III', in Z. Hawass and A. Milward Jones (eds.), *Abstracts of Papers, International Congress of Egyptologists, Cairo 28.03-03.04.2000.* Cairo: American University in Cairo: 133.

Parkinson, R. and L. Schofield
1995 'Images of Mycenaeans: a recently acquired painted papyrus from el-Amarna', in W.V. Davies and L. Schofield (eds.), *Egypt, the Aegean and the Levant: Interconnections in the Second Millennium BC.* London: British Museum Press: 125-6.

1997 'A painted papyrus from Amarna', in J. Phillips (ed.), Ancient Egypt, the Aegean and the Near East: Studies in honour of Martha Rhoads Bell, I. San Antonio: Van Siclen: 401-6.

Persson, A. W.
1942 *New tombs at Dendra.* Lund: C.W.R. Gleerup.

Peterson, S.E.
1981 Wall Paintings in the Aegean Bronze Age: The Procession Frescoes. Ph.D. thesis, The University of Minnesota, [#]82-11524.

Pusch, E.B.
1985 'Ausländisches Kulturgut in Qantir-Piramesse', in S. Schoske (ed.), *Akten des 4 internationalen Ägyptenkongresses, II. Munich.* Hamburg: Buske: 249-56.

Rehak, P.
1995 'Enthroned figures in Aegean art and the function of the Mycenaean megaron', in P. Rehak (ed.), *The Role of the Ruler in the Prehistoric Aegean.* Aegaeum 11. Liège and Austin TX: 95-118.

1999 'The Mycenaean "Warrior Goddess" revisited', in R. Laffineur (ed.), *Polemos. Le contexte guerrier en Égée à l'Âge du Bronze.* Aegaeum 19. Liège and Austin TX: 227-37.

Robins, G.
1997 *The Art of Ancient Egypt.* Cambridge, Ma.: Harvard University Press.

Rodenwaldt, G.
1921 *Der Fries des Megarons von Mykenai.* Halle: Niemeyer.

Schofield, L. and R.B. Parkinson
1994 'Of Helmets and Heretics: a possible Egyptian representation of Mycenaean warriors on a papyrus from el-Amarna', *Annual of the British School at Athens* 89: 157-7.

Schofield, L. and R.B. Parkinson
1995 'Of Helmets and Heretics: Mycenaeans on a painted papyrus from Amarna', *Bulletin of the Institute of Classical Studies* 40: 241.

Smith, W.S.
1965 *Interconnections in the Ancient Near East: a study of the relationships between the arts of Egypt, the Aegean and Western Asia.* New Haven: Yale University Press.

1981 *The Art and Architecture of Ancient Egypt.* Harmondsworth: Penguin.

Taylour, W.
1969 'Mycenae 1968', *Antiquity* 43: 91-7.

Touchais, G.
1999 'La Grèce continentale au début du bronze récent (environ 1650-1450 av.J-C)', in A. Caubet (ed.), *L'acrobate au taureau. Les découvertes de Tell el-Dab'a (Égypte) et l'archéologie de la Méditerranée orientale (1800-1400 av. J-C)* Paris: Musée du Louvre: 197-222.

Vermeule, E.T.
  1975 *The Art of the Shaft Graves at Mycenae.* Cincinatti: University of Oklahoma Press.

Wace, A.J.B. and C.W. Blegen
  1939 'Pottery as evidence for trade and colonisation in the Aegean Bronze Age', *Klio* 32: 131-47.

Wachsmann, S.
  1987 *Aegeans in the Theban Tombs.* Orientalia Lovaniensia Analecta 20. Leuven: Peeters.

Weatherhead, F.
  1992 'Painted pavements in the Great Palace at Amarna', *JEA* 78: 179-94.
  1995 'Wall-paintings from the King's House at Amarna', *JEA* 81: 95-113.

Younger, J.G.
  1995 'Aegean seals and other Minoan-Mycenaean art forms', in W. Müller (ed.), *Sceaux Minoens et Mycéniens. Corpus der Minoischen und Mykenischen Siegel, Beiheft 5.* Berlin: Gebr. Mann Verlag: 331-48.

THE AGE OF THE SPHINX AND THE DEVELOPMENT OF THE GIZA NECROPOLIS

Colin Reader

Introduction

The research on which this paper is based has largely been undertaken in response to the work of the American geologist, Robert M. Schoch, who in the early 1990's published a paper which concluded that the Great Sphinx of Giza was significantly older than was generally thought.[1] Schoch reached this conclusion following a study of the limestones from which the Sphinx was carved. In these rocks he saw evidence for erosion by rain.

In Schoch's view there had not been any substantial rains in Egypt since the end of a post-glacial wet phase which ended circa 5000 B.C. Furthermore, Schoch argued that the limestones exposed during the construction of his early Sphinx would require a period of time to degrade. This, claimed Schoch, pushed the date for the construction of the Sphinx beyond 5000 B.C. – possibly to 7000 B.C.

This early date was anathema to Egyptologists, who conventionally date the construction of the Sphinx to the Fourth Dynasty reign of Khafre (ca. 2500 B.C.). As Egyptologists were quick to point out, there is no archaeological evidence to support the early date for the Sphinx that had been proposed by Schoch[2]. The people of Egypt from ca 5000 B.C. were known to archaeologists as hunter-gatherers; people who did not have the capability to work stone on such a monumental scale.

Schoch's case was weakened further by a number of geologists who had been working in Egypt and who put forward mechanisms of weathering that, they felt, allowed the degradation of the Sphinx to be explained within a time-frame that was consistent with the conventional age of the monument. These mechanisms generally relied on processes of chemical weathering, by which moisture in the air is able to remove soluble salts from the exposed limestone. Such salts were shown to be abundant in the strata from which the Sphinx was carved, strata which extend across most of the Giza Plateau.[3]

Chemical weathering and other agents of degradation, such as abrasion by wind-blown sand, have undoubtedly influenced the degradation of the Sphinx. As has been discussed in a previous paper, however, these processes are not able to account for all the features of degradation that are present within the Sphinx enclosure (the low-lying area in which the Sphinx sits). It has been argued that, in addition to the processes of weathering and erosion that have been cited by others in support of the Fourth Dynasty date for the Sphinx, additional processes of degradation have modified the exposed limestones.[4]

The nature of these additional processes is discussed in the present paper, which summarises the author's previously published work and explores a number of other, previously unpublished, issues.

The attribution of the Sphinx to Khafre – the location of the Sphinx

In order to support the attribution of the Sphinx to the Fourth Dynasty pharaoh, Khafre, it has been argued that the Sphinx was carved from a block of limestone, left-over from quarrying undertaken during the reign of Khufu.[5] If this were the case, it provides an earliest possible date for the construction of the Sphinx (i.e. not before the reign of Khufu). It has also been argued that, as an integral part of Khafre's mortuary complex, the site of the Sphinx was dictated by the layout of adjacent features, such as the Sphinx Temple, Khafre's valley temple and Khafre's causeway.[6] Both these arguments, however, tend to neglect the influence of natural processes on the development of the Giza Plateau.

The 'quarry-block' hypothesis assumes that original ground levels at Giza were above the level of the head of the Sphinx and were reduced by extensive Fourth Dynasty quarrying. Quarrying on this scale would, however, represent a gross modification to the Giza landscape and is not consistent with the extent of quarrying that has been established by archaeological investigation[7] nor with the geomorphological evidence that can be gathered from the site.

Aigner, identified that the Giza area had been inundated by a landward advance of the Mediterranean sea during the Pliocene (2-7 million years ago).[8] The erosion caused by this inundation was controlled largely by the south-easterly dip of the Upper Mokattam Limestones and resulted in the formation of the plateau, much as we see it today, bounded by a number of north and eastward facing raised cliffs.

---

[1] Schoch, 1992.
[2] Hawass et al, 1994, 45.
[3] Gauri et al, 1995.
[4] Reader, 2001.
[5] Reisner, 1942, 26.
[6] Lehner et al, 1994, 32.
[7] Lehner, 1985a, 121.
[8] Aigner, 1983, 318.

Colin Reader

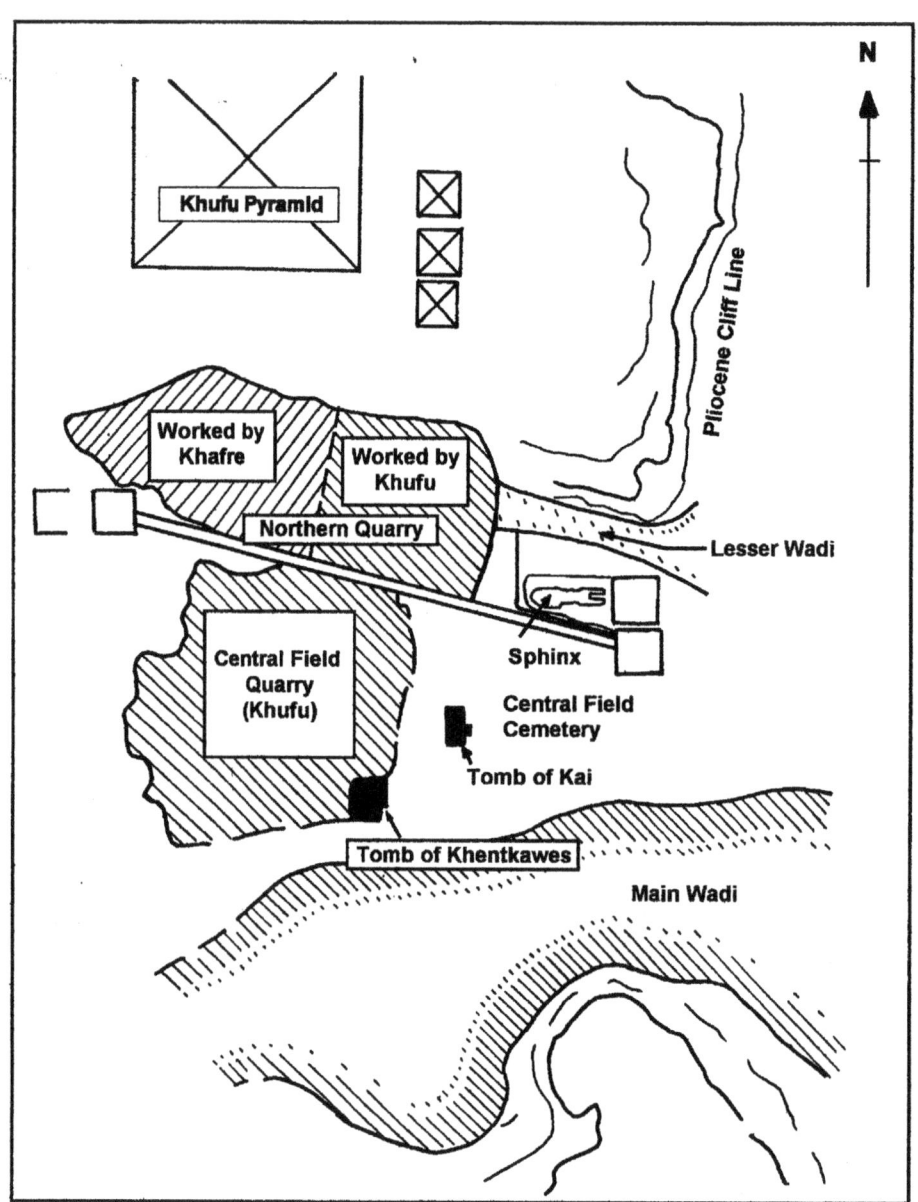

Fig. 1. Sketch plan of the central area of the Giza Necropolis.

In addition to the evidence presented by Aigner, there are a number of features which are relevant to the issue of the location of the Sphinx. To the south of the Giza necropolis is the 'Main Wadi', with the area between the Main Wadi and the Sphinx occupied by a number of tombs, the eastern part of the Central Field Cemetery (Fig. 1). Although the Central Field area has been modified by ancient quarrying and construction, it is possible to discern the original ground profile running through the lower part of a number of tombs and rising to the north and west towards the Sphinx.

To the north of the Sphinx, a modern tourist road runs east/west along the foot of a rock face into which a number of tombs have been cut. The state of weathering and erosion of this rock face, and its continuity with the Pliocene cliff line that defines the eastern limit of the Giza Plateau, indicates that this is a naturally eroded feature, which is considered to be the northern bank of a second smaller wadi (the 'Lesser Wadi'– Fig. 1). The presence of this Lesser Wadi has been independently identified by others.[9]

Rather than support the hypothesis that the position of the Sphinx was controlled by the presence of existing temples and other structures, collectively, these geomorphological features indicate that the development of the area surrounding the Sphinx was determined on the basis of the local topography. Originally, ground levels rose from the Main Wadi in the south, to a high point in the vicinity of the Sphinx. The mass of rock from which the Sphinx was later to be carved, was isolated from the northward continuation of the plateau (the area of

---

[9] El-Baz, 1992, Figure 4.

Khufu's pyramid) by the Lesser Wadi. The resulting outlier, capped by durable Member III strata is likely to have preserved the steepened profile of the Pliocene cliff line on its eastern flank and, consequently, may have been particularly prominent when viewed from the Nile valley.

The geology and degradation of the Sphinx

The limestones from which the Sphinx has been carved have been divided into three principal units or members.[10] The lowest lying rocks, the Member I strata, consist of a massively bedded reefal limestone. The Member I rocks form much of the floor of the Sphinx enclosure and both the lower part of the enclosure walls and body of the Sphinx. The overlying Member II rocks are by comparison, rather thinly bedded, consisting of a series of thirteen alternating harder and softer limestone beds. The Member II strata make up most of the body of the Sphinx and the southern and western enclosure walls. Above the Member II rocks, the head and neck of the Sphinx are carved from the Member III strata – perhaps the most durable of the exposed limestone units.

Concentrating on the Member II beds, chemical weathering has affected the softer beds to a greater degree than the more durable units. The resulting degradation, as discussed by Gauri[11], has taken the form of a pattern of near-horizontal banding, with the more durable beds projecting from the weathered face. This horizontal banding can clearly be seen on the body of the Sphinx (Fig. 2).

As Gauri noted, this banded degradation extends, relatively uniformly, across all four sides of the Sphinx.[12] It can also be observed along the eastern sections of the southern wall of the Sphinx enclosure, however, this banded degradation differs markedly from the pattern of degradation along the same limestone beds exposed in the western enclosure walls. What appears to have previously gone unnoticed is that in the west of the enclosure, the horizontal degradation reaches greater depth, resulting in the more durable beds protruding further from the cut face. Most significantly, however, these limestone beds are cut by deeply incised sub-vertical features, with the strata between the vertical features having a heavily rounded appearance (Fig. 3). These features of degradation, which are restricted to the western walls of the Sphinx enclosure, are considered to represent more intense degradation and, as such, they are particularly significant for the debate on the age of the Sphinx.

In response to these issues, a number of people have argued that it *may* be possible to explain the variation in degradation described above in terms of chemical weathering, with factors such as aspect and the position of the exposures with respect to groundwater movement thought to play a key role.

The issue of aspect can be readily addressed. The western enclosure walls (Fig. 3) and the chest of the Sphinx (Fig. 2) are exposures with the same aspect, both facing east towards the rising sun. It is evident that, whereas the degradation of the chest of the Sphinx is characterised by features described by Gauri in relation to chemical weathering, the degradation of the western enclosure wall is markedly different.

As well as sharing a common aspect, there are a number of other cut faces at Giza that are in a similar hydrogeological setting to the Sphinx. None of these, however, show even incipient development of the rounded degradation, which characterises the western Sphinx enclosure.

Fig. 2. Degradation of the eastern elevation of the Sphinx. Author's photograph.

---

[10] Gauri, 1984.
[11] Gauri, 1981.
[12] Gauri et al, 1995, 127.

Colin Reader

Fig. 3. Degradation of the western wall of the Sphinx enclosure. Author's photograph.

The degradation of the walls in the western end of the Sphinx enclosure has few, if any, parallels within the Giza Necropolis. Furthermore, the processes responsible for this anomalous degradation had, over a scale of tens of metres, a selective or restricted effect on the exposed limestone beds, a characteristic, which is not generally associated with chemical weathering or sand abrasion. It is argued, therefore, that the development of this characteristic degradation requires the action of processes of erosion or weathering in addition to those that have been cited in support of the Fourth Dynasty date for the Sphinx.

The surface hydrology of the Giza Plateau

The Sphinx sits at the low lying edge of the sloping Giza Plateau, a location that is vulnerable to erosion, not from rainfall itself as Schoch advocated, but from rainfall run-off - a process that, in the right conditions, will follow heavy rain. Heavy rains are known to have been experienced throughout Egyptian history, with the resulting run-off leading to choking of tombs in the Valley of the Kings and, at Giza, to late Old Kingdom damage of mudbrick structures, as Reisner found at Menkaure's valley temple.[13] Indeed Lehner has provided evidence of run-off within the Sphinx enclosure, in the form of a shallow drainage channel eroded into the rocky enclosure floor.[14]

The Giza Plateau rises from the former limit of Nile flooding in the east, to a watershed some 600 m west of the pyramid of Khafre, a catchment of over 1.5 km. Heavy rain falling on the fine grained rocks of the plateau is likely to have led to saturation of the ground surface, leading in turn to the discharge of the excess water downslope. In the vicinity of the Sphinx, such run-off will have discharged over the western walls of the enclosure eroding the limestone surface and scouring any exposed joints.

Independently, Selwitz has remarked on the contribution of heavy rainfall to the erosion of the Sphinx, having observed what is presumably small scale run-off discharging along erosion channels exposed at the surface. The same author notes, however, that "This analysis has to be viewed against meteorological data which indicates that between 1931 and 1981, annual rainfall averaged only about 25mm a year." [15] The implication of this is that, although the geomorphology of the exposed limestones supports the principle that the Sphinx has been subject to erosion by rainfall, the current climatic conditions do not support such a theory.

When attempting to reconstruct the history of the Sphinx, it is important to note that simply using the present climatic conditions as a key to understanding the historic degradation can be misleading. Available data indicates that before the late Fifth Dynasty, conditions in Egypt were generally wetter than at present, suggesting that

---

[13] Reisner, 1931, 44.
[14] Lehner, 1992, Figure 10.

[15] Selwitz, 1990, 857.

before this time, increased annual rainfall will have been encountered.[16] Although not the heavy, sustained rains of 7000 to 5000 B.C. cited by Schoch,[17] the wetter conditions before the late Fifth Dynasty are likely to have been characterised by a seasonal rainfall distribution. Seasonal run-off from the plateau with its associated erosion, will have been separated by more arid conditions in which chemical weathering will have continued to degrade the exposed faces. This cyclical pattern of weathering and erosion will have rapidly led to the selective degradation of the western Sphinx enclosure walls and, it is argued, the development of a pattern of degradation which is fully consistent with what can be observed on site.

As both the climatic data and the late Fifth Dynasty flood damage to Menkaure's valley temple at Giza demonstrate, however, the erosion of the Sphinx by rainfall run-off does not, in itself, require any reconsideration of the Fourth Dynasty age of the Sphinx.

Fourth Dynasty development at Giza

Although rainfall over an intact Giza Plateau is likely to produce a substantial volume of run-off, the natural surface drainage of the plateau was severely disrupted in the early Fourth Dynasty by quarrying undertaken for the construction of the pyramids.

A short distance upslope of the Sphinx enclosure is the eastern limit of a quarry worked, according to Lehner, during the reign of Khufu (Fig. 1). [18] The presence of this quarry can be seen today as a rubble and sand filled depression.

Quarrying on this scale will have had a significant impact on the surface hydrology of the plateau, with the open quarry simply intercepting any run-off from the higher ground in the west. The permeability of the backfill that eventually accumulated within the quarried depression, is likely to have been too great for the generation of any significant run-off. Even when backfilled, therefore, the quarry will have acted as a soak-away, intercepting run-off from the higher plateau in the west. The effect of this quarrying, therefore, will have been to protect the Sphinx from further run-off from up-slope, bringing an end to the erosion of the western enclosure walls.

That the characteristic erosion of the western Sphinx enclosure is attributable to the effects of rainfall run-off is consistent with the pre-quarrying topography of the Giza Plateau. Furthermore, no other process of weathering or erosion has yet been identified which can fully explain both the distribution of the degradation within the Sphinx enclosure and the fact that these features of more intense degradation are, otherwise, generally absent from the necropolis. The anomalous degradation of the Sphinx enclosure must, it is argued, have developed before the Fourth Dynasty quarrying began, when run-off generated across an intact Giza Plateau, was able to discharge downslope, over the western walls of the Sphinx enclosure.

It is concluded, therefore, that the construction of the Sphinx pre-dates the construction of Khufu's pyramid complex and the associated quarrying.

The evidence of the sphinx Temple

There is, however, further geoarchaeological evidence to suggest that the conventional age of the Sphinx may need to be re-assessed. By far the most compelling evidence for a pre-Fourth Dynasty date for the original construction of the Sphinx comes from a low excavation into the Member I limestones, which run around the base of the Sphinx enclosure, to the north and west of the Sphinx.

Generally, this cut face exhibits significant degradation, however, at a point opposite the north fore-paw of the Sphinx, there is an abrupt change in the condition of the exposure (Fig. 4). From this position to a point that aligns with the eastern face of the Sphinx Temple, the exposed limestone exhibits comparatively little degradation.

This little-degraded face was cut, according to Lehner[19] in the Fourth Dynasty, probably to facilitate a northward extension of the Sphinx Temple, part of a second phase of Sphinx Temple construction.[20] The comparative lack of degradation along this Fourth Dynasty excavation, clearly identifies it as a later cutting into an existing excavated face. The more intense degradation of the limestone beyond this Fourth Dynasty excavation indicates not only the greater age of the original excavation of the Sphinx, but also illustrates the relatively benign influence of post-Fourth Dynasty chemical weathering on these particular Member I beds.

There is, therefore, a strong geological case to indicate a pre-Fourth Dynasty age for the construction of the Sphinx. But is it necessary to consider the early Sphinx as an isolated structure or is there evidence that the Sphinx was part of wider development at Giza?

Pre-Fourth Dynasty development at Giza

Studies of the fossil assemblage of the limestones from which the Sphinx was carved have shown that the masonry used to construct the Sphinx Temple was quarried from within the Sphinx enclosure, strengthening

---

[16] Butzer, 1971, 32.
[17] Schoch, 1992.
[18] Lehner, 1985a, 124.

[19] Lehner et al, 1980, 16.
[20] Ricke, 1970.

Colin Reader

Fig. 4. The western limit (arrowed) of the Fourth Dynasty excavation (foreground) in Member I rocks within the Sphinx enclosure. Note the more heavily degraded Member I strata (background). Author's photograph.

Fig. 5. Tombs, with architecture typical of the Fourth Dynasty at Giza, built against the east-facing façade of the tomb of Kai. At the position arrowed, the niched façade of the tomb of Kai had undergone significant degradation before apparently Old Kingdom tombs were constructed. Author's photograph.

the argument made above that the two monuments were built at the same time. The same studies, however, were unable to establish with any certainty the source of the stone used in the construction of Khafre's valley temple.[21]

Khafre's causeway and the southern Sphinx exposure share a common alignment, suggesting that the two features may be of the same age. Does this common alignment suggest that, like the Sphinx, the causeway may also pre-date the Fourth Dynasty?

Khafre's causeway was not built from masonry but was actually quarried from *in situ* limestone and, therefore, excavated from the plateau itself. The development of the causeway is, therefore, linked to the quarrying of this area of the plateau. The northern quarry has already been referred to, in relation to the effect of quarrying on run-off and on the age of the Sphinx. Lehner has argued, however, that in order to satisfy demand for stone, Khufu extended quarrying into the Central Field area, to the south of what later became Khafre's causeway (Fig. 1).[22]

Under the conventional chronology, however, in which the reign of Khufu pre-dates that of Khafre, this sequence of quarrying appears to provide an additional anomaly. The development of quarrying reported by Lehner requires us to accept that Khufu's workmen went to the trouble of opening up a second quarry rather than remove the ridge of limestone which forms Khafre's causeway. The difficulty with this hypothesis is that, at the time of Khufu's development, two reigns before Khafre, this causeway would have served no known purpose.

My interpretation of the actual sequence of development at Giza, however, is that the causeway was present, or at least the alignment of the causeway was established, before Khufu began the construction of his pyramid complex. Under this scenario the causeway limited the extent of the later quarrying works.

At the western end of the causeway is Khafre's mortuary temple and, with respect to this structure, two issues are particularly notable. Firstly the temple is built in two distinct architectural styles, the western end of the temple is constructed from low, well-squared, typically Old Kingdom blocks and, in plan, much of the temple is open space. By contrast, the eastern end of the temple is only some 40% open space and is constructed in large, poorly-squared, cyclopean masonry.

Also notable is that the cyclopean masonry is built on one of the highest points on the Giza Plateau, with ground levels falling away gently to the west, towards Khafre's pyramid, and sharply to the east, towards the Sphinx. In fact, the cyclopean portion of the mortuary temple is built on a more prominent location than even Khafre's pyramid; being situated on a low knoll that before the construction of the pyramid occupied a prominent position on the western Giza skyline.

On the basis of these observations it is argued that, like the Sphinx, Sphinx Temple and the alignment of Khafre's causeway, the cyclopean portion of the mortuary temple (the proto-mortuary temple) also pre-dates Khufu's development of the site.

There is one other feature that adds some weight to this grouping of structures. A feature that is shared by the Sphinx Temple and proto-mortuary temple and, to my knowledge, by no other temple at Giza. When building the Sphinx Temple, it was necessary to excavate up to 3 m into the sloping plateau to form a level floor. Rather than excavate the floor and then build internal walls from mudbrick or masonry, the lower courses of the walls in the west of the Sphinx Temple were fashioned from the *in situ* limestone strata – in effect these walls were carved out of the plateau itself as the excavation of the Sphinx Temple progressed. Other than the Sphinx Temple, the only other location where this architectural technique has been noted is in the eastern part of the proto-mortuary temple.

Towards an absolute date for the sphinx and associated structures

The use of stone in the Sphinx and associated structures, suggests that whoever undertook this construction had developed a competence in working stone and most significantly, with respect to the Sphinx Temple and proto-mortuary temple, a competence in the working of stone masonry. It is proposed, therefore, that the use of stone masonry in Egypt can be used to establish a timeframe into which the pre-Fourth Dynasty development at Giza can be placed.

Recent excavation at Helwan suggests that by the late First or early Second Dynasty, skills had developed in the use of stone in tomb construction.[23] On a larger scale, masonry was used in the construction of the Gisr el Mudir, which most probably dates from the Second Dynasty.[24] On the basis of the distribution of degradation within the Sphinx enclosure and the known use of stone masonry in Egypt, the excavation of the Sphinx and the construction in stone of the associated temples is tentatively dated to the second half of the Early Dynastic Period (Early Dynastic Period being the 1st-3rd Dynasties). However, other than a number of peripherally located Early Dynastic mastabas, such as Petrie's First Dynasty Mastaba 'T', located to the south of the necropolis[25], the Giza Plateau is not generally considered to have been a site of any importance until

---

[21] Lehner, 1985b, 140.
[22] Lehner, 1985a, 121.
[23] Köhler, 1998.
[24] Mathieson et al, 1997.
[25] Petrie, 1907.

Khufu began the construction of the Great Pyramid in the Fourth Dynasty. Other than the evidence cited already in this paper for the age of the Sphinx and associated structures what, if any, evidence is there for pre-Fourth Dynasty activity at Giza?

Artefacts from what may be late Predynastic burials have been found at Giza, close to the Great Pyramid.[26] Wilkinson discusses this evidence, arguing that material of this type, from the Maadi culture of Lower Egypt, has been found at a number of locations in the Memphite area. Stating that "Although most of the sites are situated on the east bank of the Nile...there are recent indications that the west bank too was used for settlement and/or burial in the Pre-dynastic period." He then goes on to substantiate this by adding "Excavations within the modern settlement of Giza for the Cairo Waste Water Project uncovered a number of pottery vessels of the 'Maadi Cultural Complex'...confirming that Giza witnessed at least a limited degree of activity long before the Fourth Dynasty."[27] Although written to challenge the claim for pre-Fourth Dynasty development at Giza, Wilkinson's conclusion actually offers some support for the assertion that Giza was in use and, it is argued, a site of at least local importance during the Early Dynastic Period.

Given the extensive Fourth Dynasty construction activity that took place at Giza, however, it should not be surprising that few Early Dynastic monuments have survived. Large areas of the necropolis were cleared down to the limestone bedrock to allow the construction of pyramids, temples and mastabas. Areas not set aside for construction were selected for quarrying. These are both rather destructive activities and will have left little of the plateau undisturbed.

In the 1970's, excavation in the south of Giza encountered tipped debris, which had been cleared from the area of the pyramids during the Old Kingdom construction.[28] This debris was found to contain late Pre-Dynastic, First, Second and Fourth Dynasty material. Further evidence that there was Early Dynastic activity at Giza may, however, come from within the necropolis itself, particularly the Central Field area.

Both the lower rock-cut element of the Khentkawes tomb and the nearby rock cut mastaba of Kai[29] (Fig. 1) bear two groups of features that are of considerable interest for the present discussion. Firstly, these two tombs are remarkable in that, like few other exposures at Giza, the upper limestone beds are cut by features of erosion which resemble those on the western Sphinx enclosure walls. It is considered that these features were formed before the large scale Fourth Dynasty development of the site disrupted the pattern of surface drainage upslope of these tombs.

Remarkably, on these two tombs, the features of probable pre-Fourth Dynasty erosion are accompanied by a second set of features which also suggest an Early Dynastic origin for this construction. On the lower walls of these rock-cut tombs are the remains of niched or palace façade decoration, a typically Early Dynastic architectural device.

The niched façade features on the tomb of Khentkawes have been recognized by others,[30] and are limited to the lower part of the southern wall of the tomb, facing the Main Wadi. Given that, in its completed Fourth Dynasty state, the Khentkawes tomb was faced throughout with a limestone casing, which will have obscured the rock-cut niches, it is argued that the niched façade was part of an Early Dynastic development, which was usurped for the Old Kingdom burial of Khentkawes.

In the case of Kai, the remains of the niched facade extend along the southern and eastern faces of the superstructure, facing both the Main Wadi and the Nile valley itself. When compared with the tomb of Khentkawes, the excavated niches on the eastern face are better preserved, extending to a greater height up the external walls of the tomb. This better preservation can be readily explained; it is the result of protection from degradation provided by a number of tombs constructed against the eastern face of the mastaba.

Unlike the Early Dynastic architectural style represented by the niched façade, these additional tombs are characterised by the austere architectural style adopted throughout the Giza Necropolis in the Fourth Dynasty. An assessment of the eastern face of the mastaba of Kai suggests that the original rock cut tomb, with its niched façade, had been completed and exposed to degradation for some time before the addition of the overlying Old Kingdom construction. In places it can be seen that the niched façade had undergone significant degradation before the Old Kingdom masonry was added (Fig. 5).

Conclusion

The Sphinx was regarded by the ancient Egyptians as the guardian of the gates of the underworld on the eastern and western horizons, the points of sun-rise and sunset. According to Edwards[31] this association dates back to remote antiquity and suggests, it is argued, a solar association for the early Sphinx and associated structures. For example, situated on the western Giza skyline, the proto-mortuary temple was perhaps linked to the setting sun. Was it Giza's established link with worship of the rising and setting sun that led Khufu to build his pyramid

---

[26] Mortensen, 1985.
[27] Wilkinson, 2001, 161.
[28] Kromer, 1978.
[29] Hassan, 1932, 31.
[30] Maraglioglio and Rinaldi, 1967, 170.
[31] Edwards, 1993, 122.

at the site, at a time when the sun god, Re, was achieving national prominence? If so, this may explain the name the ancient Egyptians gave Khufu's pyramid, for they called it "the pyramid at the place of sunrise and sunset"[32] a name which accords with the role of the site as discussed in this paper.

The Sphinx complex may not, however, have been the only Early Dynastic development at the site. The evidence for other structures that may pre-date the Fourth Dynasty is mounting, however, given the scale of the Fourth Dynasty development of the site, little further evidence may be forthcoming. The nature of the major construction projects undertaken during the reigns of Khufu, Khafre and Menkaure may mean that the legacy of this earlier activity has, to a large degree, been removed from the archaeological record.

Cited Works

Aigner, T.
    1983 'A Pliocene Cliff Line Around the Giza Pyramids Plateau, Egypt', *Palaeogeography, Palaeoclimatology, Palaeoecology* 42: 313-322.

Baines, J. and J. Malek,
    1980 *Atlas of Ancient Egypt*. Oxford: Equinox.

Butzer, K.W.
    1971 *Environment and Archaeology: An Ecological Approach to Prehistory*. Chicago: University of Chicago Press.

Edwards, I.E.S.
    1993 *The Pyramids of Egypt*. London: Penguin.

El-Baz, F.
    1992 'Environmental Considerations in the Conservation of the Sphinx', in F.A. Esmael (ed.). *Proceedings of the First International Symposium on the Great Sphinx*. Cairo: EAO Press, 223-250.

Gauri, K.L.
    1981 'Deterioration of the Stone of the Great Sphinx', *Newsletter of the American Research Centre In Egypt* 114: 35-47.
    1984 'Geologic Study of the Sphinx', *Newsletter of the American Research Centre In Egypt* 127: 24-43.

Gauri, K.L., J.J. Sinai & J.K. Bandyopadhyay.
    1995 'Geologic Weathering and its Implications on the Age of the Sphinx', *Geoarchaeology* 10 (2): 119-133.

Hassan, S.
    1932 *Excavations at Giza, Vol 3, 1931-1932*. Cairo: Cairo Government Press.

Hawass, Z and M. Lehner.
    1994 'Remnant of A Lost Civilization?', *Archaeology* 47 (5): 44-47.

Köhler, E.C.
    1998 'Excavations at Helwan – New Insights into Early Dynastic Masonry', *Bulletin of the Australian Centre in Egypt* 9: 65-72.

Kromer, K.
    1978 'Siedlungsfunde Aus Dem Fruhen Alten Reich in Giseh. Osterreichische Ausgrabungen 1971 –75', *Osterreichische Akademie Der Wissenschaften Philosophisch-Historische Klasse Denkschriften* 136.

Lehner, M.
    1985a 'The Development of the Giza Necropolis - The Khufu Project', *MDAIK* 41:40-141
    1985b 'A Contextual Approach to the Pyramids', *Archiv fur Orientforschung* 32: 135-158.
    1992 'Documentation of the Sphinx', in F.A. Esmael (ed.). *Proceedings of the First International Symposium on the Great Sphinx*. Cairo: EAO Press, 55-107.

Lehner, M., J.P. Allen and K.L.Gauri.
    1980 'The ARCE Sphinx Project - A Preliminary Report', *Newsletter of the American Research Center In Egypt* 112: 3-33.

Lehner, M and Z. Hawass.
    1994 'The Sphinx:Who Built it and Why?', *Archaeology* 47 (5): 32-41.

Maragioglio, V. and C. Rinaldi.
    1967 *L'Architettura delle piramidi Menfite, part VI*, Rapallo.

Mathieson, I., E. et al.
    1997 'The NMS Saqqara Survey Project 1993-1995', *JEA* 83: 17-54.

Mortensen, B.
    1985 'Four Jars From the Maadi Culture found at Giza', *MDAIK* 41: 145 to 147.

Petrie, W.M.F.
    1907 *Gizeh and Rifeh*. London: Egypt Research Account.

Reader, C.D.
    2001 Geomorphological Study of the Giza Necropolis, with implications for the development of the site', *Archaeometry* 43(1): 149-159.

Reisner, G.A.
    1931 *Mycerinus, the temples of the Third Pyramid at Giza*. Cambridge, Mass.: Harvard University Press.
    1942 *A History of the Giza Necropolis I*. Cambridge, Mass.: Harvard University Press.

Ricke, H.
    1970 'Der Harmachistempel des Chefren in Giseh', *Beitrage zur Agyptischen Bausforschung und Altertumskunde* 10: 1-43.

Schoch, R.M.,
    1992 'Redating the Great Sphinx of Giza', *KMT* 3 (2): 53-59 & 66-70.

---

[32] Baines and Malek, 1980, 140.

Selwitz, C.
 1990 'Deterioration of the Great Sphinx: an assessment of the literature', *Antiquity* 64: 853-9.

Wilkinson, T.A.H.
 2001 'Comment on C.D. Reader, "A Geomorphological Study of the Giza Necropolis, with implications for the development of the site"', *Archaeometry* 43 (1): 161-163.

THE TRANSITION TO STATE SOCIETY IN EGYPT: PROBLEMS AND POSSIBILITIES OF APPLYING MORTUARY EVIDENCE

Joanne Rowland

Abstract

A relational database and Geographical Information System (GIS) is being employed to house data pertaining to mortuary remains from four Predynastic/Early Dynastic sites in the Nile Delta: Kafr Hassan Dawood, Kufr Nigm, Minshat Abu Omar and Tell Ibrahim Awad.

The system is intended to facilitate investigations of inter- and intra-site configurations. Preliminary results suggest both a likely increase in differentiation at an intra-site level, in grave contents and in the spatial distribution of graves (as well as regional distribution of sites), together with a degree of decrease in differentiation at the inter-site level as the centralisation which accompanies the arrival of state society begins to emerge.

Introduction

The current research is concerned with the period of transition to state society in Egypt. The area from which the data is being considered is the Nile Delta, in an attempt to redress the balance of Predynastic research in favour of this region, since to date a far greater proportion of work has been undertaken in the Nile Valley, both in terms of excavation and analysis.

The research aims to look at the social transformation occurring in Egypt during this important transitional period, especially the transition from the indigenous Delta, Maadi-Buto cultures to the Naqada culture of Upper Egypt. One long-term research aim is to discuss and test existing models of state formation through the examination of both intra-site and inter-site relationships within the Delta region.

The data come mainly from mortuary contexts and comprise both published and unpublished material. The author has access to the unpublished records from the east Delta sites of Kafr Hassan Dawood and Kufr Nigm, and is consulting the published material on Minshat Abu Omar and Tell Ibrahim Awad. These sites are located in the eastern Delta and their proximity to each other is shown in Fig. 1.

The sites of Kafr Hassan Dawood, Kufr Nigm, Minshat Abu Omar and Tell Ibrahim Awad vary in their length of occupation, however, they all cover the crucial period from the terminal Predynastic to the Early Dynastic period. Of these four sites, the two most thoroughly excavated to date, in terms of the mortuary contexts, are Kafr Hassan Dawood (situated on the bank of the Wadi Tumilat) and Minshat Abu Omar (on a gezira). Kufr Nigm and Tell Ibrahim Awad are partially excavated, and much of the excavation at the latter site has focussed on later periods of activity, which are continuous from the period being considered here, through the Old Kingdom and on to the New Kingdom. The other three sites have evidence from the Predynastic/Early Dynastic phase, with a subsequent break until the evidence that is associated with the Late Period and Ptolemaic Period.

To aid in the collation of the data from these sites, the methodology of a computerised database system, linked to a Geographical Information System (GIS) is being utilised. The initial data set employed for this methodological model has been from Kafr Hassan Dawood, and a set of standard criteria has been implemented for the collation of information from the other sites. The use of data in this form is intended to facilitate comparative analysis and data manipulation to test various hypotheses, and the different types of data held within the system include grave location, grave contents, human remains, grave construction, and presence of specific features such as potmarks, and *serekhs*.

The purpose of this paper is to address some problems and possibilities that might be associated with utilising sets of mortuary data to interpret changes in social differentiation. Due to the constraints of space and time, I have chosen in this text to discuss a model relating to differentiation on an intra-site level and to refer to the material from the two most completely excavated sites in terms of mortuary evidence, Kafr Hassan Dawood and Minshat Abu Omar.

Intra-site

When considering the evidence from the perspective of a single site, it is necessary to consider how the increase in centralisation and social differentiation, that might be expected to accompany the rise of complex society, may be reflected in the mortuary remains. It is important to stress here that ethnographic studies prove that there are aspects of the funerary ritual that express the status of the individual, which are not preserved in the mortuary record.[1] The prestige accorded an individual may be equally shown through the ability of the deceased to 'mobilize' drink, food and guests for the wake and that these 'constitute the main forum for the display and reinforcement of status, rather than the burial and grave goods'.[2] To begin with, a model must be formed to project how the organisation of society might be affected

---

[1] David 1992.
[2] David 1992, 198.

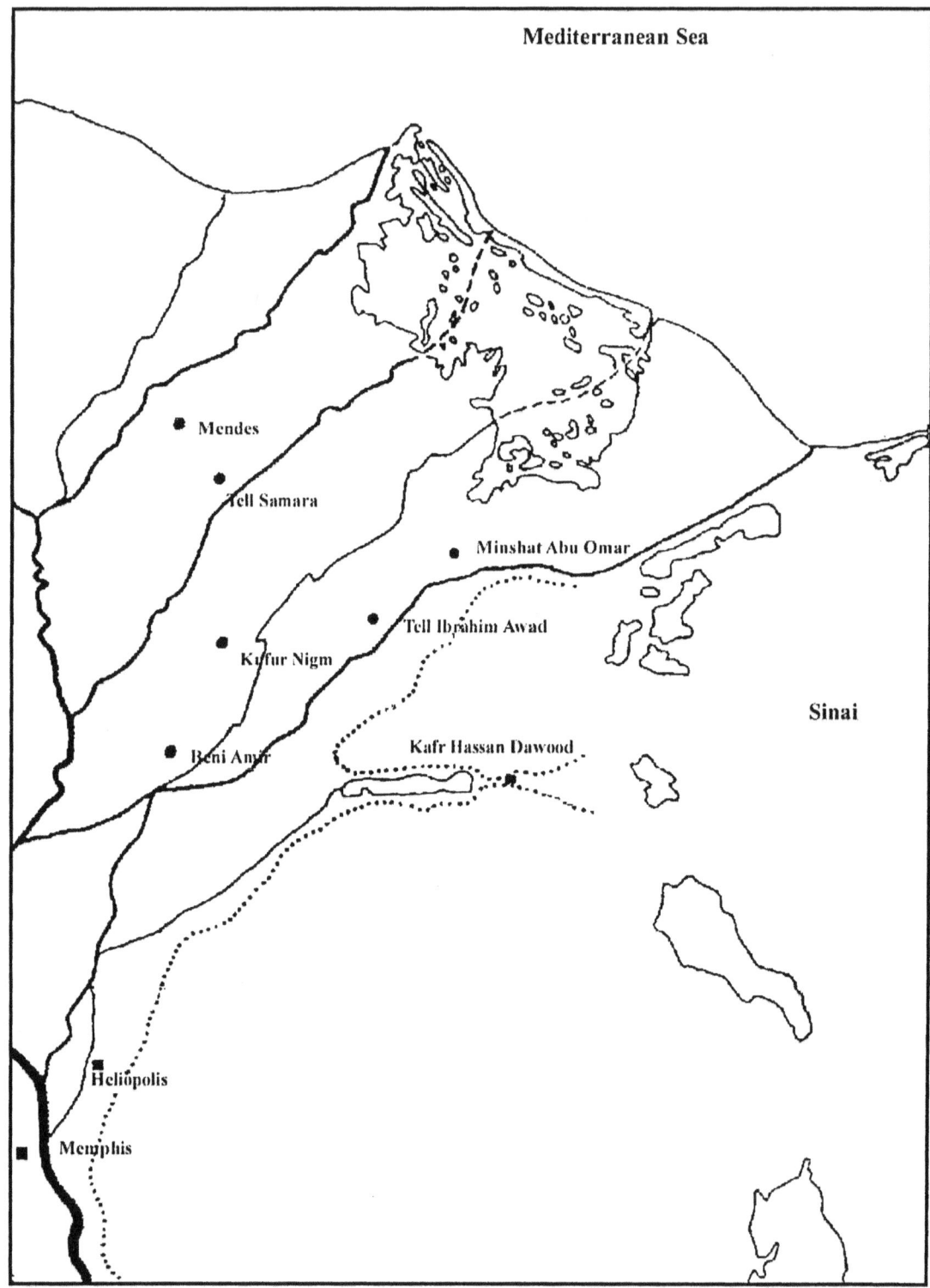

Fig. 1. Map of site locations in the east Delta. Drawing by G. J. Tassie.

and, consequently, how this might be reflected in mortuary practice.

This working model proposes the following: that with the rise of complexity it will be possible to witness increasing tiers of status differentiation within the community. This will be visible in terms of the distribution of wealth, and the differentiation of wealth within age and sex subgroups. A declining correlation between age, sex, and the position of the individual within the society may also be observed.[3] It is vital to assess whether such differentiation is suggestive of an egalitarian, ranked or stratified society, each level being associated with increasing complexity,[4] and to clarify whether burials suggest acquired or inherited wealth. Where the data suggests that grave contents/construction correlates to the age and sex of the deceased, then it is likely that the community has an egalitarian basis, and that differentiation in status is achieved throughout life. However, where the data suggests that there is no such correlation, i.e. that child burials are as well provided for as adult burials, then this suggests that status is acquired through birth. Where a relatively small number of larger/higher status burials exist, it might be suggested that it is a ranked society, with one chief or big man,[5] operating at a time, whilst a larger number might suggest a stratified society with differing kinship-based castes. It is also worth pointing out Fried's comments that certain individuals within a ranked society may be providing for others on an increasing scale, thereby "creating obligations" among the recipients, and that this may create a problem in the mortuary data, in as much as a position of elevated status has no material correlate.[6] Correspondingly, he emphasises the importance within a stratified society, of the correlation between economic status, and social status and in equality[7].

When a Terminal Predynastic/Early Dynastic cemetery site is being considered it might be expected that as the cemetery develops, temporally, a greater amount of differentiation might accompany this development. It must be noted, however, that the temporal spread might not follow a logical pattern and deviations might exist for a number of reasons. Ucko warns that some studies have erred in as much as "they focus attention on the chronological implications without considering the possible form of social processes which must have been involved".[8]

From a different angle, Goldstein discusses how changes in mortuary evidence may appear to reflect changes in social organisation, or the presence of differential ranking. She cautions however, that such differentiation may be representative of temporally changing attitudes to the funerary ritual, and warns that it is unreliable to suggest that all cultures "will ritualise a particular aspect of their social organisation in the same form".[9] Parker Pearson echoes Goldstein's warning, that two burials made during different periods of cemetery use may appear to reflect very different social statuses, whereas the prosperity of the site given a during period might be wholly responsible for this phenomenon.[10]

Within the mortuary context, it is possible to examine

a) the content of the graves
b) the construction of the graves
c) the spatial distribution of graves within the cemetery

Within these parameters, it may be beneficial to consider such issues as

i) distribution of wealth across a site, or rather variation in grave assemblages/construction
ii) whether wealth/status may be acquired or inherited: this may be investigated through such means as age, quantity of tombs reflecting higher wealth/higher position in society
iii) treatment of the body
iv) spatial location of graves
v) differentiation being reflected through a number of different subgroups: male/female, child/adult

At Kafr Hassan Dawood, excavations show a temporal development of the cemetery from the north to the south of the site, with more dense use of the space in the north (Fig. 2, GIS plan of the Terminal Predynastic/Early Dynastic cemetery). The northernmost extremity of the site is still awaiting excavation during the next season. As shown in Fig. 3, preliminary spatial analysis of the cemetery site has shown that in the north of the site there is a higher proportion of simple, oval grave pits (1.1 x .8 m), whereas, rectangular graves are to be found in the north and south of the site, with the two largest graves excavated to date in the far south. These graves are numbered 913 (shown) and 970 and measure approximately 6 x 4 m each.

At Minshat Abu Omar, the Late Predynastic graves are mainly oval pits, and the Early Dynastic graves are "generally rectangular, and ... larger and deeper than the earlier ones".[11] Castillos notes further, in Egypt as a whole, that, "after Early Predynastic times there was a marked increase in the number of people occupying small tombs matched by a corresponding decrease in the number of those buried in medium-size and larger

---

[3] Johnson and Earle 2000, 126.
[4] Fried 1967.
[5] Johnson and Earle 2000, 211-13.
[6] Fried 1967, 115.
[7] Fried 1967, 52 & 188-9.
[8] Ucko 1969, 276.

[9] Goldstein 1981, 56-7 & 61.
[10] Parker Pearson 1999, 85.
[11] Kroeper in Bard 1999, 529.

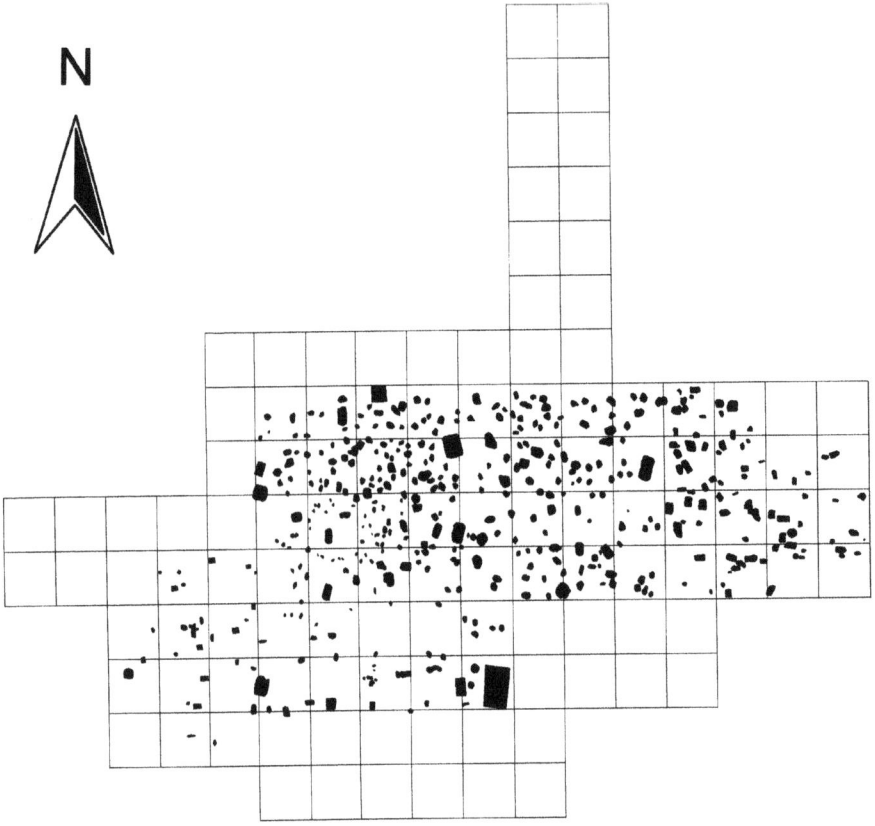

Fig. 2. GIS plan of the Terminal Predynastic/Early Dynastic Cemetery at Kafr Hassan Dawood.

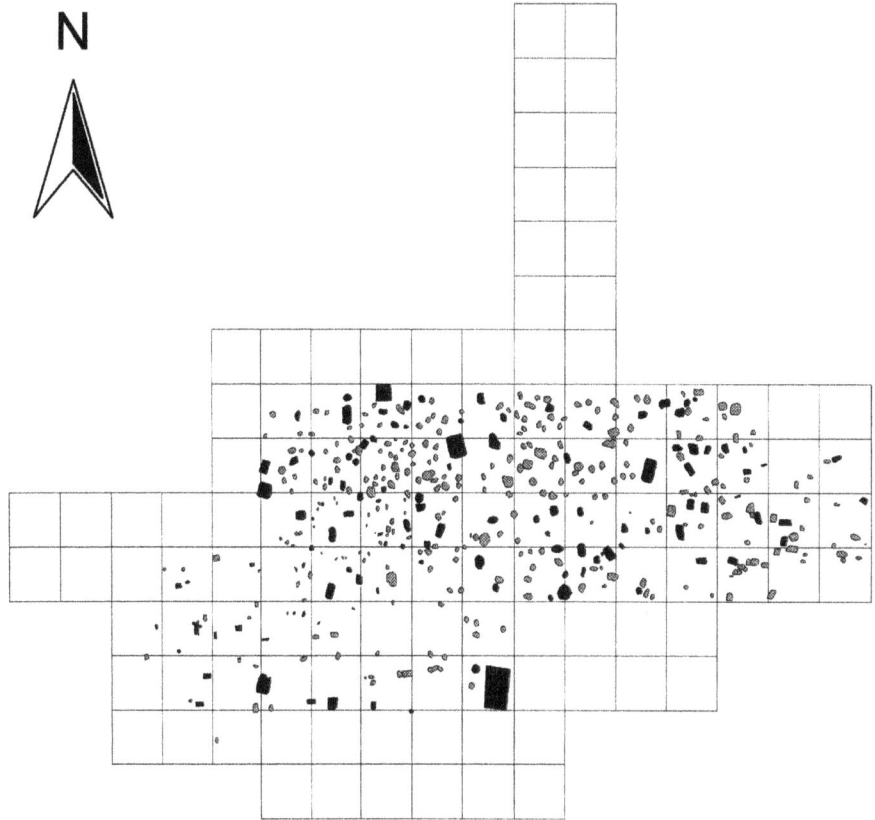

Fig. 3. GIS plan of the Early Cemetery at Kafr Hassan Dawood, showing the distribution of oval and rectangular graves.

graves", and notes the differentiation in wealth in terms of, "a significant increase in wealth reflected by the dramatic rise in the number of richly endowed tombs" and points to the, "appearance of wooden or pottery coffins".[12]

At Minshat Abu Omar, in contrast to Kafr Hassan Dawood, there is a temporal development from the south to the north of the cemetery, with augering suggesting the presence of a settlement contemporary to the early cemetery to the southeast.[13] In the south there are shallow pits with few grave goods; in the centre of the site, deeper, richer graves are located, which are less densely distributed than the shallow pits in the south; and in the north of the site are the graves with the finest wares, this also being where *serekhs* containing the names of kings have been located. Here, in the north of the site are eight burials that have been classified by the excavation team as elite and which are dated to the Early Dynastic Period/end of Dynasty I. These graves fall within the groups of those classified (in terms of assemblage and construction) to MAO III and IV. The Minshat Abu Omar material is classified chronologically and typologically into groups I-IV by burial tradition, ceramics, and other grave goods. Groups III and IV include those graves where there is increasingly elaborate treatment in terms of grave construction and where an extra chamber is introduced for the placement of grave goods, especially to house the larger vessels included within the assemblage.

The development in grave architecture at Minshat Abu Omar is from simple oval pits with few goods in the Late Predynastic, to larger, rectangular, chambered pits (including some burials with coffins) in Dynasty 0, to the area containing eight elite burials in Dynasty I. At Kafr Hassan Dawood, there is a comparable development, and indeed there is also the occurrence of coffins although here they are of oval shape and made of pottery. There have been nine such located to date, the most recent in the far south of the site, grave 1025, shown in Fig. 4, and it is notable that three coffins have been located within one 10m grid square in the south of the site.

At Kafr Hassan Dawood there are no tombs that are directly comparable to the elite eight tombs from Minshat Abu Omar. The richest and most elaborately constructed tombs at Kafr Hassan Dawood, of which there are two, have been found in the far south of the cemetery. These tombs are 913 (excavated by the Supreme Council of Antiquities) and 970 (excavated by the University College London-Supreme Council of Antiquities team). These two tombs date to the reign of King Narmer. Both of these tombs contain in excess of eighty artefacts, and are by far the largest tombs in the cemetery. Grave 970 contains wine jars of the type represented by the MAO IV assemblages and Early Dynastic beer jars. Of note,

however, are two tombs which have been located in the earlier, northern, part of the cemetery. These are tombs 1008 and 1041,[14] which have been dated to the reigns of King Sekhen (Ka) and Aha, respectively. In grave 1008 a *serekh* of King Sekhen was found on a storage jar that is comparable to a jar from Helwan dated to Naqada IIIa1-c2 (IID2-IIIC1), and grave 1041 has been dated to Aha based on the pottery assemblage.[15] Grave 1008 is oval in shape and is the largest oval grave in the cemetery, at 1.8 x 1.5 m. Within the grave are seven different types of artefact, comprising a total of thirty two objects, the same number of different types as seen in tomb 913, and grave 1008 also contains the largest number of artefacts found in an oval grave. The grave contents include fine pottery and two imported vessels and the ceramics are representative of two phases of pottery, with vessels of MAO assemblages III and IV. Grave 1041, only contains fifteen grave goods, of two types of artefact, and is a rectangular grave, some 2.2 x 1.43 m. This grave contains ceramics and a copper chisel, and although placed amongst the earliest burials at the site, it represents the latest burial located to date, from the Terminal Predynastic/Early Dynastic cemetery.

This evidence reflects the points raised concerning visibility of differentiation in the mortuary record and also raises some problematic issues. The content of the graves, to an extent, correlates with their construction; the tombs with the most elaborate architecture tend to also be those with the highest number and greatest variety of grave goods. In the early stages of site development at Kafr Hassan Dawood, the graves appear to represent greater uniformity and in the later stages, there is far greater evidence for social differentiation. Graves 913 and 970 stand out, and while they must clearly represent individuals of some status within the community, the problem exists as to whether they provide evidence for differentiation within a ranked or stratified society. The low number of graves of high status might be more suggestive of a ranked society, with the presence of only one 'chief' at a time.

Insufficient bioanthropological data presents a great problem. At Kafr Hassan Dawood, for example, only a small proportion of the 744 burials in the early cemetery have been examined by bioanthropologists, which severely hampers the possibility of distribution patterns being associated with age and/or sex. All that can currently be said is that out of those graves where sex has been discerned, the largest (sexed) grave belongs to a male (2.2 x 1.7 m) and the largest female grave is 1.6 x 1.3 m. The male grave contains five vessels (three ceramics, two stone) and the female grave contains no objects.[16] This admittedly small group of sexed graves does not suggest that any particular artefacts are associated with either male or female burials at Kafr

---

[12] Castillos 1982, 174.
[13] Kroeper in Bard 1999, 531.

[14] Hassan 2000, 39.
[15] Hassan 2000, 39.
[16] Rowland 1998.

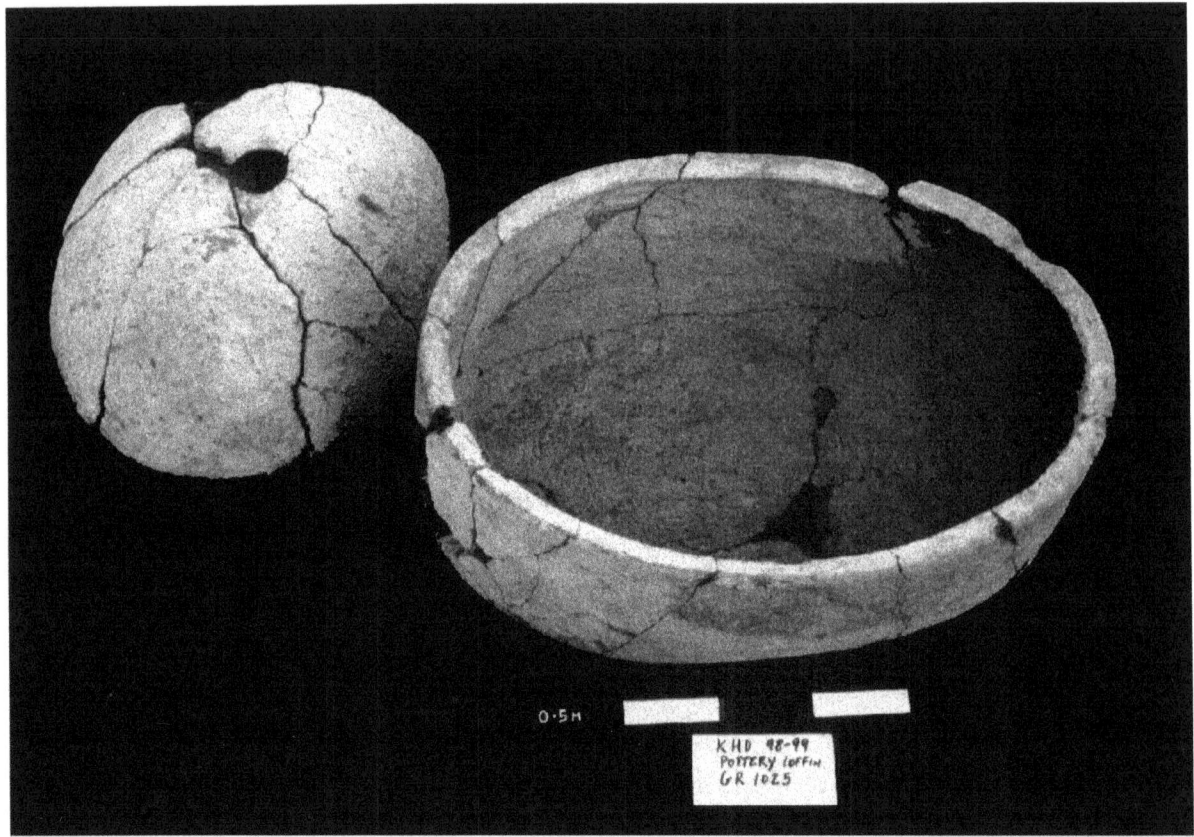

Fig. 4. Pottery coffin from grave 1025 at Kafr Hassan Dawood. Photograph by Ken Walton, reproduced courtesy of Professor Fekri Hassan.

Hassan Dawood. At Minshat Abu Omar, however, there is an apparent association between the sex of the interred and certain artefacts, for example in graves accorded group IIIb status, where the presence of jewellery is associated with female burials, and in group IV, cosmetic jars and a bone cosmetic box are found in association with female burials.

Conclusion

The model outlined above is intended to highlight different problems and possibilities that might arise when examining mortuary evidence for signs of differentiation in the living society. This paper has concentrated on an intra-site level, but it is also important to look at the evidence from other perspectives, and at different scales. Inter-site analysis, which will be a part of forthcoming research, will consider how differentiation between sites might be affected by the rise of complexity. Deductions concerning large-scale social transitions cannot be assumed from evidence derived from a single site and comparisons will be drawn with the other sites in the field of my research, and beyond. Looking to the evidence from sites elsewhere in Egypt at this period will help to make inferences on the type of social and political organisation within Lower Egypt and the extent to which this is influenced by the Nile Valley culture. This comparative research will be facilitated by the use of the standard criteria structure of the database for statistical analysis and the GIS for spatial analysis.

Acknowledgements

The investigations at Kafr Hassan Dawood have been funded by UNESCO, the National Geographic, the Bioanthropology Foundation, The Supreme Council of Antiquities, Uppsala University, The Humanities Research Council of Canada and the Institute of Archaeology, University College London. My Ph.D. research is being funded by the British Academy AHRB. Thanks go to Prof. Fekri Hassan for allowing me access to the Kafr Hassan Dawood and Kufr Nigm material, and for his continued support. My thanks also go to Dr. Kevin MacDonald for his comments on this paper.

Joanne Rowland
University College London

References Cited

Bard, K. A.
    1988 'Quantitative Analysis of the Predynastic Burials in Armant Cemetery 1400-1500', *JEA* 74: 39-55.

Castillos, J. J.
  1982 *A Reappraisal of the Published Evidence on Egyptian Predynastic and Early Dynastic Cemeteries.* Toronto: Collection of papers.

David, N.
  1992 'The archaeology of Ideology: Mortuary Practices in the Central Mandara Highlands, Northern Cameroon', in J. A. Sterner and N. David (eds.). *An African Commitment: Papers in honour of Peter Lewis Shinnie.* Calgary: University of Calgary Press: 181-210.

Fried, M. H.
  1967 *The Evolution of Political Society.* New York: Random House.

Goldstein, L.
  1981 'One-dimensional archaeology and multi-dimensional people: spatial organisation and mortuary analysis', in R. Chapman, I. Kinnes and K. Randsborg (eds.). *The Archaeology of Death.* Cambridge: Cambridge University Press.

Hassan, F. A.
  2000 'Kafr Hassan Dawood', *Egyptian Archaeology* 16: 37-9.

Johnson, A. W. and T. Earle.
  2000 *The Evolution of Human Societies.* Stanford: Stanford University Press.

Kroeper, K.
  1999 'Minshat Abu Omar', in K. A. Bard (ed.). *Encyclopedia of the Archaeology of Archaeology of Ancient Egypt.* London: Routledge: 529-31.

O'Shea, J. M.
  1996 *Villagers of the Maros – A Portrait of an Early Bronze Age Society.* New York: Plenum Press.

Parker Pearson, M.
  1999 *The Archaeology of Death and Burial.* Texas: A&M University Press.

Rowland, J. M.
  1998 *An Analytical Study into the Distribution of Wealth at the Egyptian Predynastic Cemetery Site of Kafr Hassan Dawood.* Unpublished M.A. thesis, University College London.

Ucko, P.
  1969 'Ethnography and archaeological interpretation of funerary remains', *WA* I (1969/70): 262-80.

SINGLE MOTHER GODDESSES AND DIVINE KINGSHIP: THE SIDELOCK OF YOUTH AND THE MATERNAL BOND

Geoffrey Tassie

Introduction

The modes of body decoration that people use send out signals on many different levels; some are socio-sexual, others may be ritualistic. The hairstyles of Egyptian deities send out signals of a cosmological and social nature. The behaviour of the deities in both myth and ritual can also be seen as setting ethical codes for social behaviour, modelling the social norms that should be aspired to, as well as grounding and reinforcing political and economic developments. At the centre of the Egyptian cosmogony was divine kingship, which also defined Egyptian society in its own image. Women as goddesses in association with royal ideology were often analogous with giving birth, nursing and protection.[1] When the hairstyles of deities are transferred to humans they reinforce the social bonds established in the cosmological myths. The distinctive hairstyle of children, the sidelock of youth is just such a hairstyle, although it has rarely been studied fully (see fig. 1).

The Evolution of the Sidelock of Youth

Originally the sidelock may have been worn by Predynastic Egyptian warriors,[2] in a similar manner to the Libyan and Asiatic warriors,[3] although this is uncertain. However, the rare depictions of children in the Predynastic Period, all show them with a bald head, and normally being held by their mother.[4] In the Early Dynastic Period children are again rarely depicted, but when they are shown, they are again portrayed as bald and nude, although now they are often in the classic finger to mouth pose.[5]

At the start of the Old Kingdom, the sidelock, which appears to have developed as an adult style throughout the Predynastic and Early Dynastic Periods, started to be worn by children, although the completely shaved head remained a popular style for younger children. The sidelock was usually placed on the right side of the head, and consisted of a lock of shoulder length hair, with the rest of the hair being either cropped or completely shaved. This rise in the popularity of the sidelock being worn by children seems to coincide with the rise to prominence of Hathor, one of the sky-goddesses. Hathor's popularity appears to have increased from being a minor deity to a state goddess, alongside, and probably as a consequence of the elevation of the sun-god Re. For, by Dynasty III, Hathor was recognised as the wife of Re,[6] although by the end of the Old Kingdom she seems not to be affiliated to any god in particular. Throughout Dynasties II, III and IV, Re ascended to ultimate supremacy amongst the deities, being incorporated into kings' names, and in Dynasty IV, during the reign of Djedefre, the epithet 'Son of Re' was added to the royal titulary.

The style of the lock changed through time; originally, it was a narrow plait with the end rolled up in an outward facing curl, usually worn on the right side of the head. This style remained popular for both boys and girls during all periods, even when, in the latter part of the Old Kingdom, girls started to wear backlocks and pigtails with discs attached to the tips. This continued when multi-locks started to be worn by both girls and boys during the Middle Kingdom. The thickness and method of dressing the sidelock also changed through time. During the New Kingdom very thick sidelocks were worn, sometimes left loose, sometimes plaited. Multi-tufts also begin to be sported during the New Kingdom.[7] However, the sidelock of youth in its various forms remained the most popular hairstyle for children from the Old Kingdom through to the Late Period.[8] However, the dressing of children's hair in this manner may have been

---

[1] Hassan 1992, 307, suggests that the older myths and rituals were concerned with birth, death and resurrection, and that these rites of passage were associated with goddess cults. In Hassan 1998, *passim,* he argues that the earliest Egyptian goddesses were associated with birth, nursing and protection, especially of the king.

[2] On a fragment of a ceremonial palette from late Nagada III, a warrior wearing a penis sheath is shown smiting an enemy. He is depicted with what appears to be a bald-head apart from four crosshatched tresses, which hang to his breast. There appears to be no front or back section to this hairstyle, leading to the conclusion that it is a sidelock being depicted. However, the origin of the warrior is uncertain, Schäfer, 1986, Pl. 3.

[3] Hittite, Libyan and Hamathite warriors all wore locks of hair as a sign of valour, Corson 1965, 26-31 and also Hölscher 1955, 34-35. In Europe the ancient Germans, such as the Chatti, never clipped their hair or beards until they had slain an enemy, Frazer 1922, 232. A similar code existed among young Aztec warriors 'a man who failed to participate in the capture of even one prisoner was not allowed to cut off the lock of hair that all youths were required to wear - so this became a lasting source of shame and humiliation for him', Trigger 1993, 67.

[4] One such Predynastic figurine is the Nagada I baked clay figurine (BM 58066) of a mother holding two babies, now in the British Museum, which shows the mother as nude with long hair, and the babies as nude and bald, Hornblower 1929, Pl. VII.1. Another mother and child figurine, this time made of ivory again shows them as both bald, Smith, & Simpson 1981, 29. A Nagada II-III figurine, now in the Berlin Museum, shows a mother holding her infant on her hip. Both the mother and infant are shown nude, the mother with long swept back hair, the baby with no hair, Strouhal 1992, 22-23. A Nagada III figurine portraying a mother and baby in buff pottery shows the mother as topless with a skirt on and the child as nude, both are shown as bald, Aldred 1965, 29.

[5] This pose of children is noted for the Early Dynastic Period, Fletcher 1995, 105-111.

[6] Tower Hollis 1995, 49.

[7] The chronological development of children's hairstyles is given in Fletcher 1995, *passim* and Janssen & Janssen 1990, 37-8.

[8] Fletcher 1995, *passim.*

Fig. 1. Suckling scene showing King Unas being suckled by his 'mother' in the guise of a goddess. King Unas' mother cradles the young king with her forward arm and offers her breast with the other arm so that the King can take her nipple between his lips. From the Pyramid Temple of Unas, Saqqara, Dyn. V. Drawn by Claire F. Venebles.

just a custom of the elite, for when children of the rest of society are depicted in the nobles' tombs, they are shown with either shaved or cropped heads (see fig. 2).

Sidelocks found on mummies of young boys and girls prove that they were indeed worn and were not just artistic convention. At Mosteggeda, four boys were found with sidelocks, all dating to Dynasty V or VI. In three cases, the sidelock was worn on the right side of the head but in one case, the sidelock was worn on the left side.[9] In the valley of Deir el-Medina a prince of Dynasty XX, aged about five years, was found in his coffin, which had been abandoned there during a removal of coffins from the Valley of the Queens; the prince, possibly a son of Ramesses III, still wears the sidelock on the right side of his head. Another prince, aged about eleven, found in the tomb of Amenhotep II (KV. 35), and possibly one of the king's sons, also still had his sidelock attached to the right side of his head.[10] Sometimes good luck charms such as fish or other cultic amulets were suspended from the tip of the lock to give protection to the wearer, especially during the Old and Middle Kingdoms.[11]

The Aetiology of the Sidelock and the Mythogenesis of Horus

The sidelock of youth was called the *srt* or Horus lock. The wearers of the sidelock were called *ḥnsktyw*.[12] Another word for a wearer of the sidelock was *dȝw*, 'hairy one'.[13] The symbol of the lock of youth could also stand on its own as a hieroglyph meaning child, or act as the determinative in the word for child *ḥrd*. The lock of hair was emblematic of a 'son' in imitation of the youthful god Horus, the son of Isis and Osiris, who was held forth as a virtuous role model for all children; it also invoked the protection of Horus. But why was Horus

---

[9] Brunton 1937, 105.
[10] Janssen & Janssen, 1990, 38.
[11] Andrews 1990, 171-3.
[12] Faulkner 1962, 173. It is possible this term actually refers to a class priestesses of Hathor who wore a triple braid; this interpretation forms part of the ongoing research.
[13] Breasted 1906, 190.

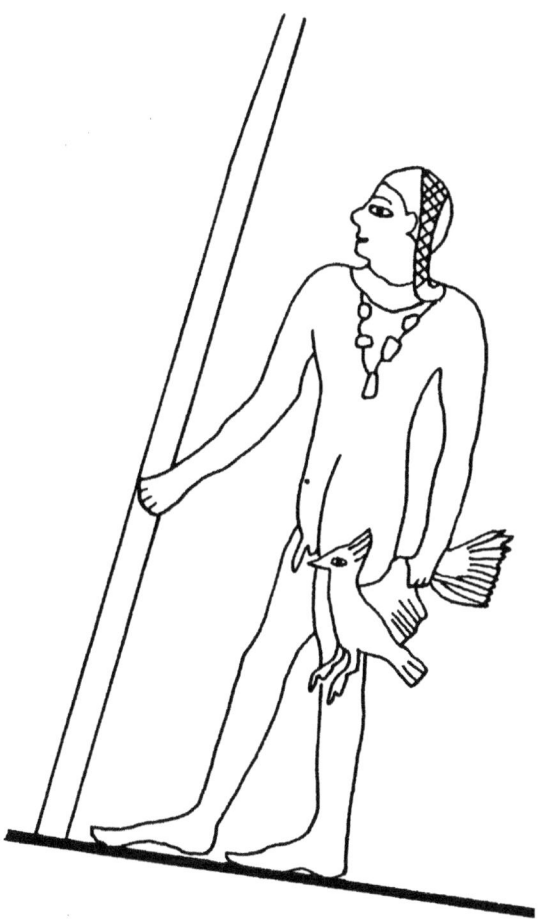

Fig. 2. A traditional plaited sidelock of youth on the son of Ptahhotep. Adapted from the reliefs in the mastaba of Ptahhotep, Saqqara, Dyn. V. Drawn by Claire F. Venables.

shown with a sidelock? What role did it perform mythically or symbolically?

At the beginning of the Old Kingdom, before the rise of the Heliopolitan and other popular theogonies, Horus was regarded as the son of Re and Hathor.[14] One of the king's early titles was 'Son of Hathor',[15] Hat-hor meaning 'House of Horus'.[16] Although a more literal reading of Hathor's name may be taken to mean 'Womb of Horus', the seat of power, fulfilling the functions of fertility, nourishment and protection, and also as the sky goddess, the playground of Horus.[17] However, Hathor started to give way to Isis in the late Old Kingdom, when the legend started to be absorbed into the Osirian myth, requiring Horus to become the son of Osiris and Isis in order to further legitimate the king's claim to the throne as the personification of Horus, by bringing the king into the familial Osiride myth.[18]

Hathor, as the original single mother bringing up Horus in the marshlands at Khemmis, is usually shown suckling the neonate in the form of the *ihet* cow.[19] Hathor's role in nurturing and protecting the young Horus made her an ideal deity to protect all mothers and their young children, as well as being a maternal role model.[20] In the more expansive Heliopolitan myth of Isis and Osiris, it was Isis as a single mother who raised Horus in the town of *Akh-bity* (Khemmis) in the Delta marshes, protecting him from his father's brother, Seth. On reaching maturity, Horus went out into the world to avenge his father's death at the hands of Seth.[21] However, the Osirian myth also includes the conception of Horus, which took place after Isis had gathered all fourteen parts of her husband Osiris' body that Seth had hidden in various places around Egypt. In one version of the myth, *The Contendings of Horus and Seth,* Isis lays Osiris on a bed and then turns into a kite and breathes life into her dead husband with her wings. Isis then uses magic to reawaken Osiris' 'weary member' and places herself on it, thus conceiving Horus.[22] In Plutarch's *Iside et Osiride*, a fish ate Osiris' phallus and so Isis made a replacement out of wood to which she gave life, enabling her to conceive Horus.[23] Osiris went on to become the 'Lord of the Underworld' and Isis raised Horus on her own in the Delta marshlands. However, Isis still continued to protect Horus even after he had started on his 'manly' quest to avenge his father and claim the throne of Egypt from Seth who had usurped it. At the end of the Horus and Seth rivalries the question of who was to rule Egypt was to be settled by a jury of the Ennead. However, Isis beguiled Seth and trapped him by subterfuge into admitting that Horus was the rightful heir to the throne of Egypt.

Hathor is often shown with an oval, featureless face, cow's ears or a bicornate headdress, suggesting the personified womb or bicornate uterus of a heifer.[24] This gynaecological symbolism seems to have been integrated into the familiar bouffant, curled up hairstyle so prominent on depictions of Hathor from the Middle Kingdom. Medusa's head in Greek mythology is

---

[14] In a juxtaposition in later mythology Hathor became known as Re's daughter and in the New Kingdom she became Horus' lover, producing a son, Ihy. Hart 1986, 76-82; Tower Hollis 1995, 49.
[15] Hart 1986, 77.
[16] Springborg 1990, 6.
[17] Springborg 1990, 135.

[18] Isis first started to be mentioned as the mother of Horus in the VIth Dynasty *Pyramid Texts*, although it is not until the Middle Kingdom that the Osirian myth including Horus becomes established. Hart 1986, 77; Tower Hollis 1995, 49-51.
[19] Robins 1995, 34.
[20] Hathor, along with the other birthing and fertility deities Bes and Taweret, were often cited in protective prayers of the mother-to-be, or new mother to protect her neonate, Robins 1993, 75-91. Birthing rooms or nurseries in houses were often decorated with images of deities, including Hathor and offerings were made at her shrines and temples for safe deliverance during childbirth, Robins 1996, 29-39.
[21] Plutarch 1970, *passim*.
[22] Manniche 1995, 54.
[23] Manniche 1995, 54.
[24] Frankfort 1944, 198-200. The catching of men with the hair of a woman is a recurrent theme in Egyptian literature, especially the lassooing of a lover, as expouded upon in the Chester Beatty Papyrus, Lichtheim 1976, 187.

Fig. 3. Hathor capital showing plaited form of typical Hathoric hairstyle. From the Temple of Bastet, Bubastis, Dyn. XXII. Author's photograph.

symbolic of female genitalia and her tangled hair represents the female pubic hair, and the terrifying female powers of entrapment.[25] Egyptologists have long associated the imagery of Medusa with Hathor's head and hair, and also with the wild-haired god of childbirth and 'birthing deity', Bes.[26] In addition to Hathor, deities such as Horus and Khonsu seem to have begun as sacred gynaecological archetypes, only latterly mythologized with the anthropomorphism of the regenerative symbols.[27] Horus represented Osiris' umbilical cord, Isis (having taken over the role from Hathor) his uterus, and Khonsu his placenta.[28] Horus as the sacred umbilical cord was also Osiris' twin or *ka*, and also the twin of the pharaoh; Khonsu was also a royal twin, being the gods', as well as all royal placentae. An important part of ancient Egyptian kingship was the concept of the eternal nature of kingship, the continuation of the institution of the monarchy. The King as the personification of Horus, the king's immortal other, along with his *ka*, was one of the central factors of the continuity of the monarchy.[29]

If Hathor's hair symbolised the primordial womb, (especially when it was plaited, suggesting the texture of the coiled neck of the womb),[30] and the side lock of youth, (again, especially when plaited), replicated the texture of the coiled umbilical cord,[31] then the hair of Hathor and Horus should be seen as symbolising the filial relationship between mother and son (see fig. 3). Horus wearing this external representation of his birth, demonstrated his love, admiration and honour for, and affiliation to his mother, Hathor. However, because of the ancient Egyptians love of dualism, the sidelock was also probably emblematic of Horus as a warrior, and at the same time symbolically represented the residing place of the *ka* of the god Osiris, protecting Horus from harm until he attained adulthood and avenged his father's death.[32] The sidelock being the residing place of the sacred *ka* and twin, also strengthened the relationship of the king as

---

[25] Slater 1992, 16-20. Particularly the sexuality of the mother, and the male (son's) fear of castration.
[26] Springborg 1990, 124.
[27] The gynaecological symbols were given full human form as deities, Springborg 1990, 124.
[28] Khonsu is often depicted sporting a sidelock: as the personification of the royal placenta-*ka*; the wearing of a hairstyle symbolic of the umbilical cord is fitting. Khonsu as a royal twin (as was Horus) is thus in his youthful form shown wearing the sidelock. Khonsu as the son of Amun and Mut would also have worn the sidelock to denote his childhood status, even though Khonsu seems to actually be an older deity, known from the Old Kingdom.

[29] Baines 1993, *passim*; Baines 1993a, *passim*.
[30] Barb 1953, 220-1.
[31] Springborg 1990, 140.
[32] In some traditional societies men who have taken a vow of vengeance sometimes keep their hair unshorn until they have fulfilled their vow. Marquesans sometimes have their head shaved, except for one lock on the crown, that either hangs loose or is tied up. They wear this latter hairstyle when they have a solemn promise of avenging a close member of the family, and only after they have fulfilled their vow do they cut the lock off, Frazer 1922, 232.

Horus, with Re, the son of the sun, and also the relationship between Horus and Osiris, who was also known as the '*Ba of Re*' from the Middle Kingdom onwards. During the day Re crosses the sky, at night he traverses the netherworld in his night form, as Osiris. The completion of the solar cycle helps to unite the Osirian myth into the solar Ennead. The sidelock can be seen as a badge of valour and legitimation, keeping the family's honour by avenging his father and being the legitimate heir to his father's inheritance – the throne of Egypt. In everyday life the symbolism of Horus' hairstyle, when worn by a mortal child, can be seen as a physical emblem of the close relationship, both physiological and psychological between mother and child, and also of the residing place of the child's *ka*, protecting them from ailments until they had reached adulthood.[33] It also displayed the role of the child as a protector and avenger, and also that they were the rightful heir to their father's inheritance.[34]

Love Thy Mother, Honour Thy Father

Very little evidence is left to us in the archaeological record about the birth or formative years of children, apart from some casual references in narratives, myths and iconography.[35] However, from the religious texts, folk tales and instructional literature it is clear that it was the mother that was the familial glue, that it was the norm for men to be married with a family, even if they worked away from home and that the father's inheritance should go to his son. However, the idiom that played the biggest role in keeping the fabric of Egyptian society from being rendered, was the duty to honour one's mother.[36] In the literature a son's duty towards his father seems to be defined by the role Horus played towards his father, Osiris; he was the protector, avenger and legal heir.[37] Common epithets from male autobiographies at the end of the Old Kingdom and in the First Intermediate Period state '*I was one beloved of his father, praised of his mother.*'[38] However, there are far more literary passages that specifically tell children to exhort their mother, one of the most poignant being the following passage from the New Kingdom text *The Instructions of Any*:

'*Double the food your mother gave you,*
Support her as she supported you;
She had a heavy load in you,
But she did not abandon you.
When you were born after your months,
Still she was yoked [to you],
With her breasts in your mouth for three full years.
And then as you grew and your excrement disgusted,
She was not disgusted, saying: 'What shall I do?'
When she put you in school,
where you were taught to write,
She kept watching over you daily,
With bread and beer in her house.
And when as a young man, you take a wife
and establish your own household,
Pay attention to your offspring,
Raise them the way your mother did [for you],
Do not give her reason to blame you,
Lest she lift her hands up to god,
And he hears her prayers.'[39]

The Sidelock of Youth in the Rites of Passage into Adolescence

Young children were sometimes portrayed as being nude[40], seeming to indicate that they lacked any real social recognition and status until they had reached social adulthood[41], although it is obvious that even neonates were considered as embodied persons, since they were named at birth.[42] Moreover, the mortuary data from Deir el-Medina seems to indicate that there were broad stages of childhood, with neonates buried furthest away from the adults, children further up the cemetery and adolescents nearest to the adults.[43] Therefore, the inscribing of Egyptian culture upon the body and the socialisation of the individual seems to be a gradual process, the first step in this process being the naming of the baby, the next stage appears to be the rite of passage that marked the child's entry into adolescence. In this rite of passage the sidelock of youth was cut off and offered to the god Horus, signifying their separation from childhood. The name for this ceremony was *ts-mdḥ* 'the tying around of the fillet', probably in imitation of Isis tying a fillet around the head of her son Horus as he set out in search

---

[33] The Toradjas believed that a child's soul resided in their sidelock. For they would shave their children's heads to rid them of head-lice, but leave a lock at the crown as a refuge for the child's soul. If the soul had nowhere to settle they believed the child would sicken and possibly die, Frazer 1922, 323-33. The Karo-Bataks also had similar beliefs, and left this lock in place until manhood, Frazer 1922, 323-33. The wearing of gold sidelock pendants seems to reinforce the protective power of the sidelock, Andrews 1990, 171-3.
[34] The Egyptian literature seems to confirm that a son's social responsibility to his father was defined by the mythical role of Horus and his relationship to his father, Osiris. This was to protect, avenge if need be, and that he was his father's legal heir, Leprohon 1999, 50-5, 85-6.
[35] Janssen & Janssen 1990, 115.
[36] Leprohon 1999, 50-5, 85-6.
[37] Leprohon 1999, 55.
[38] Robins 1993, 107.

[39] Lichtheim 1976. 141.
[40] Janssen & Janssen 1990, 26-41, have postulated that the depicting of children as nude equates with their lack of social status, since children's clothes have found. Also, in the winter months that the children would have to needed clothes in order to keep them warm, although nudity amongst children could have been practised in the summer months, it was probably artistic convention to show them as nude, particularly in the Old Kingdom, to demonstrate their lack of social status. However, it could also indicate their innocence.
[41] Janssen & Janssen 1990, 26-41; Meskell 1999, 130-1.
[42] Feucht 1995, 107; Horung 1992, 178.
[43] Meskell 1999, 172.

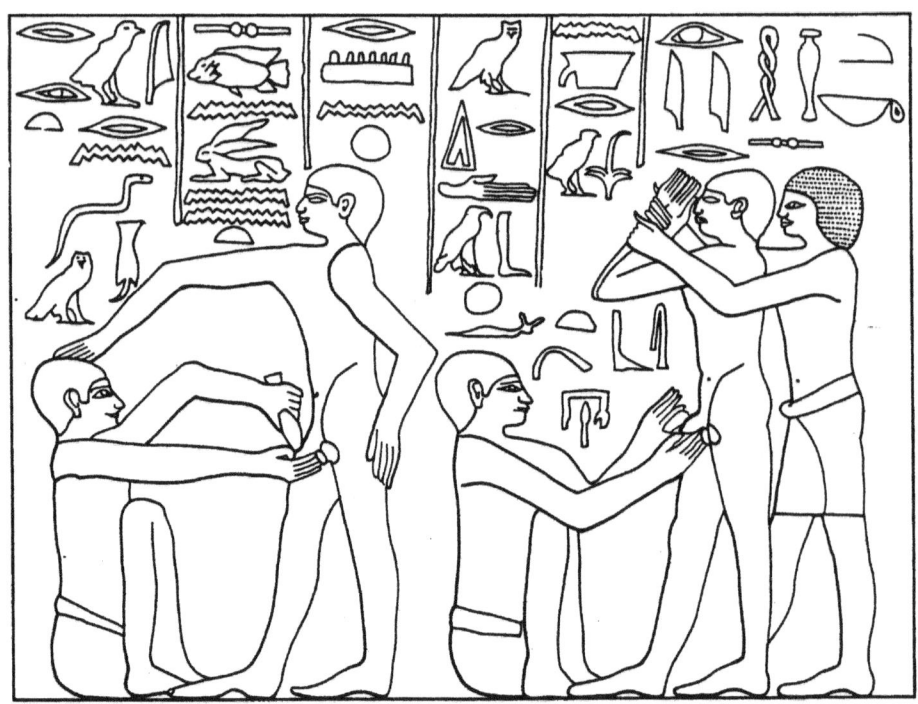

Fig. 4. Circumcision scene from the mastaba of Ankhmahor, Saqqara, Dyn. V. Drawn by Claire F. Venables, after Janssen and Janssen 1990, 91.

of Seth, the murderer of his father, Osiris.[44] This part of the ritual was probably intended to separate the youth from their childhood and its lack of status, allowing them to enter society. However, this ceremony was probably just part of a much larger initiation ritual which was often supervened by an athletic competition and by grooming and purification rituals as part of a circumcision ceremony for boys, particularly in the Old Kingdom where the *ts-mdḥ* is first mentioned.[45] In the famous circumcision scene from the Dynasty VI mastaba tomb of Ankhmahor, where a boy is shown undergoing the operation, the boy is shown with a cropped hairstyle, possibly indicating that by this stage the sidelock had already been cut off.[46] There is not a single case in the surviving human remains and iconography that shows a boy wearing the sidelock after having undergone circumcision, implying that the wearing of the sidelock was a childhood custom (see fig. 4).[47]

That boys went through an initiation ceremony is documented by both iconographic and literary sources.[48] However, the evidence for girls going through a puberty ritual is less well attested, for there is only one mention of it in the written sources,[49] and as yet, the rite has not been identified in the iconographic record. However, cross-cultural studies have shown that girls ceremonies are usually singular affairs, conducted by immediate female members of the family.[50] From the archaeological record, it seems that the boys ceremony was a large, public affair with as many as 120 participants present, as noted in the First Intermediate Period Stela of Wacha from Nag ed Dêr. This states that Wacha was circumcised along with 120 other men, and that he neither scratched nor hit

---

[44] The ritual is first mentioned in the Old Kingdom but also continues to be mentioned in the Middle and New kingdoms. However, there seem to be variations on the determinative used: in the Old Kingdom it was either the generic ⌒ (*Urk.*, I, 98, 12) symbolising the fillet or the ⌒ (*Urk.*, I, 253, 18; *cf.* also 250, 14) the axe, associated with the word *mDH/mdH* 'to hew'. The use of the axe in the writing of *Ts-mDH* probably signifies the cutting off of the sidelock of youth, the severance from childhood. In the Middle Kingdom the determinative used was usually the ⌒ or the glyph showing the same fillet from the side. In the Middle Kingdom it could also be written with the feminine ending, 't' *Ts-mDHt* (*Urk.*, IV, 38, 15) indicating that a girl had gone through the ceremony. A passage from the autobiographical inscription of Simontu, now in the British Museum (Reg. No. 828; Exh. No. 145) states: 'I was a child who tied around the fillet in the time of His Majesty (Amenemhet I). When His Majesty (Amenemhet I) had departed in peace, the King of Upper and Lower Egypt, Kheperkare (Senusret I), may he live for ever, made me a scribe...', Gunn 1939, 219-20. This mention of the going through the *Ts-mDH* in this context shows how important it was in a person's life. The tying round of the fillet is also mentioned in the following texts, but whether the *psS-kf* knife was used in the ceremony is not mentioned, Davies 1986, 401-2; Vandier 1958, 492-3; Müller 1980, 273-4.

[45] Athletic games and grooming and purification rituals are all shown in connection with circumcision scenes on the wall-reliefs from the Saqqara tombs of Ankhmahor and Khentika, Roth 1991, 65-72. Roth also notes that these games and athletic scenes that are connected to the initiation ritual, are also related to Hathor, the patroness of love and fertility, 1991, 70. The length of puberty rites, as derived from cross-

cultural studies have been found to last either from 1 to 3 days, up to 2 weeks, and in some cases up to a year, Schiegel & Barry 1979, 199-210.

[46] It seems that in the Old Kingdom, circumcision was almost universal for boys, but this does not seem to be the case in other periods where it seems to be optional unless they were in the priesthood, Janssen & Janssen 1990, 91.

[47] Janssen & Janssen 1990, 97.

[48] Roth 1991, 61-72.

[49] Sethe & Helck, 1906-58, 38, 15.

[50] Schiegel & Barry 1979, 199-210.

anyone among them whilst the operation was performed.[51] Roth suggests that the sociological puberty rites were in some cases an induction into a phyle,[52] probably to start work as a mortuary priest or in a work crew.[53] This induction into familial independence and focus on responsibility amongst the boys of ancient Egypt, cannot be shown for the girls, although it seems likely that the focus of the girls ceremony was on fertility and sexuality.[54]

Some Egyptologists have estimated the age at which these initiation rites of passage were performed at about 12 years old.[55] The average age of menarche in prehistoric societies was 16 years of age; but this did not occur at the same age amongst the earth's populations, or even among individuals.[56] Puberty rites are not necessarily triggered by the first mense, emission of sperm or by signs of pubic hair or breasts; in some societies they are quite separate, although in most societies the ceremony is performed at the first signs of genital maturation.[57] Therefore the actual age that the *ts-mdh* was performed may have been between 12 and 16 years of age, an average of 14 years may be used for sociological puberty for the ancient Egyptians.

The cutting off of the sidelock of youth in the *ts-mdh* mentioned above, may have been symbolic of the original cutting of the umbilical cord with the *psš-kf* knife.[58] However, rather than cutting the baby free from the mother's body, it is a cutting free of the child from the feminine domain and integrating them into society. It is a liberation of the child from the mother's direct protection and the rule of the nursery, and an integration into the world of men.

The *ts-mdh* was the start of the process of adulthood, not the end; it signalled the breaking away from the mother's direct control, marking the physical and symbolic transition into social adulthood, the transition from the domain of childhood into the adult world of work and marriage[59], marking a social transition from one age status to another, from childhood to adolescence. For the majority of both girls and boys there seems to have been a gradual acceptance of more adult responsibility and less representations of game playing in this stage of life.[60] Older children are often shown accompanying their parents in their daily activities on tomb scenes, although when playing games, the two sexes are rarely shown together.[61] Boys may join phyles or become apprentices and assistants appointed to their fathers or other teachers. This moment is sometimes referred to as the act of 'Knotting the Girdle', the allowance of adolescents to wear a linen girdle over the gala kilt.[62] Girls would intensify their learning from the women in the female tasks, or learning in the ritualistic arts of religion or if of royal birth possibly learning the scribal arts.

Conclusion

Using palaeoethnotrichological[63] data in an holistic approach, which utilises, ethnohistoric, ethnological, textual and physical evidence, social, religious and ritualistic aspects of ancient Egyptian life can be illuminated. Some of the salient points to come from this examination are that the mother was the familial glue, that the first major rites of passage after the birth and naming of the baby was the *ts-mdh*, where the sidelock of youth was cut off and that the hairstyles and lives of the deities helped to define Egyptian society. The major point to come out of this work is that cognisance of the reasons behind the actions and appearance of the deities gives a better understanding of ancient Egyptian society.

Geoffrey Tassie
University College London

---

[51] Roth 1991, 71. However, the physical remains suggest that circumcision does not seem to have been compulsory.

[52] A phyle is a group of people that provided part-time service on temples. Work crews, and the mortuary cults of kings and high officials. At different times in pharaonic Egypt, there were either four or five different phyles. In the Early Dynastic and Old Kingdom phyles were social institutions, whereas from the Middle Kingdom they were administrative systems, Roth 1991, 2-4.

[53] Roth 1991, 61-72.

[54] Schiegel & Barry 1979, 199-210.

[55] Janssen & Janssen 1990, 94, suggest that 12 was the age at which children went through the rites of passage and were circumcised.

[56] Hassan 1981, 127-8, reviews the ages at which menarche began in traditional and industrial societies and concludes an age range from 13.5 years to 17 years. However, he takes the average for prehistoric groups as 16 years of age. The variation in the start of the first mense has been mooted as being attributable to a high protein diet. In an experiment, girls on a high protein diet reached menarche at 12.65 years of age, girls on rich carbohydrate diet reached menarche at 14.1 years of age, while girls on a balanced diet reached it at 13.42 years of age. However, there is usually a delay of between 1-4 years called *adolescent sterility*, between the first mense and when nubility (the age at which conception is possible) is reached, averaged out at 2 years. In the !Kung San of Namibia, women who reach menarche at 16.5 years, usually give birth to their first baby at 19.5 years of age, Hassan 1981, 127-8.

[57] Gennep 1960, *passim* states that the initiation rites are not triggered by the first signs of puberty which is in accordance with Schiegel & Barry 1979, 199-210. In the Jewish religion, the *bar mitzvah* for boys and the *bat mitzvah* for girls, are celebrated at 13 years of age. This age roughly coincides with the physiological age of puberty, but this does not constitute a sociological puberty rite, for its participation is limited to religious life, and does not induce wider social recognition, or changed social status.

[58] Roth 1992, 113-47.

[59] Although very little is known of the actual marriage ceremony, it has been assumed from the lack of evidence, that this rite of passage was not such an important transition for the ancient Egyptians, and may simply have involved the couple setting up house together with the exchange of a few gifts, probably at about the age of 20 years old. However, couples were married as attested to by the marriage contracts, and titles such as 'Great Royal Wife', Nur el Din 1996, 33-8.

[60] In rural areas in modern Egypt children start to run errands from about the age of three. From seven their help becomes a little more important, but once they reach twelve they start to fulfil more essential duties, helping with their parents work and helping to look after their siblings, Janssen & Janssen 1990, 107-8

[61] Boys are usually shown playing with boys in such games as the 'Hut Game', which itself may have been part of the puberty ritual. Girls are usually shown playing or dancing with other groups of girls, away from, but sometimes in the same scene or register as the boys, Janssen & Janssen 1990, 55.

[62] Janssen & Janssen 1990, 107-8.

[63] The scientific and sociological study of ancient hair.

Cited Works

Aldred, C.
   1965 *Egypt to the End of the Old Kingdom.* London: Thames & Hudson.

Andrews, C.
   1990 *Ancient Egyptian Jewellery.* London: British Museum Press.

Baines, J.
   1993 'Kingship, Definition of Culture, and Legitimation', in D. O'Connor & D. P. Silverman (eds.), *Ancient Egyptian Kingship.* Leiden: E. J. Brill: 3-48.
   1993a 'Origins of Egyptian Kingship', in D. O'Connor & D. P. Silverman (eds.), *Ancient Egyptian Kingship.* Leiden: E. J. Brill: 95-156.

Barb, A. A.
   1953 'Diva matrix', *Journal of the Warburg and Courtauld Institutes* 16: 193-238.

Bell, L.
   1985 'Luxor temple and the cult of the royal *ka*', *JNES* 44 (4): 251-94.

Blackman, A. M.
   1916 'Some Remarks on an Emblem Upon the Head of an Egyptian Birth-Goddess', *JEA* 3: 199-206

Breasted, J. H. Jr.
   1906 *Ancient Records of Egypt: Historical Documents from the Earliest Times to the Persian Conquest,* Vols. 1-5. Chicago: The University of Chicago Press.

Brunton, G.
   1937 *Mostagedda and the Tasian Culture.* London: Bernard Quartich Ltd.

Corson, C
   1965 *Fashions in Hair: The First Five Thousand Years.* New York: Peter Owen.

Davies, N. de G.
   1900 *The Mastabas of Ptah-hetep and Akhethetep at Saqqara.* Volume 1. London, Kegan Paul.

Davies, E. N.
   1986 'Youth and Age in the Thera Frescoes', *AJA* 90: 399-406.

Faulkner, R. O.
   1969 *The Ancient Egyptian Pyramid Texts.* Oxford: Griffith Institute.
   1962 *A Concise Dictionary of Middle Egyptian.* Oxford: Griffith Institute.

Feucht, E.
   1995 *Das Kind im alten Ägypten.* Frankfurt: Campus.

Fletcher, A. J.
   1995 *Ancient Egyptian Hair: A Study in Style, Form and Function.* Unpublished Ph.D. thesis, Manchester University.

Frankfort, H.
   1944 'A Note on the Lady of Birth', *JNES,* 3: 198-200.

Frazer, J. G.
   1922 *The Golden Bough: a study in magic and religion.* Abridged version. London: Macmillian & Co, Ltd.

Gennep, A. van.
   1960 *The Rites of Passage.* Trans: M. B. Vizedom & G. L. Caffee. London: Routledge & Kegan Paul.

Gunn, B.
   1939 'A note on Brit. Muse. 828', *JEA* 25: 219-20.

Hart, G.
   1986 *A dictionary of Ancient Egyptian gods and goddesses.* London: British Museum Press.

Hassan, F. A.
   1981 *Demographic Archaeology.* New York: Academic Press.
   1992 'Primeval goddess to divine king: the mythogenesis of power in early Egyptian state', in R. Friedman & B. Adams (eds.). *The Followers of Horus.* Oxford: Egyptian Studies Publication No. 2. Oxbow Monograph 20: 307-21
   1993 'Rock art: cognitive schemata and symbolic interpretation', in G. Calegari, (ed.). *L'Arte d l'Ambiente del Sahara prehistorico: dati e interpretazioni.* Memorie della Societa Italiana di Scienze Naturali s del Museo Civico di Storia Naturale di Milano, Milano: 269-82.
   1998 'The earliest goddesses of Egypt', in L. Goodison & C. Morris (eds.) *Ancient Goddesses: The Myths and the Evidence.* London: British Museum Press: 98-112.

Hölscher, W.
   1955 *Libyer und agypter: Beiträge zur ethnologie und geschichte Liyscher völkerschaften nache den Altägyptischen quellen.* Hamburg: Verlag J. J. Augustin

Hornblower, G. D.
   1929 'Predynastic figures of women and their successors', *JEA* 15: 35-47

Horung, E.
   1992 *Idea into Image: Essays on Ancient Egyptian Thought.* New York: Timken.

Janssen, R. M. & J. J. Janssen.
   1990 *Growing up in Ancient Egypt.* London: The Rubicon Press.

Leprohon, R. J.
   1999 'The Concept of Family in Ancient Egyptian Literature', *KMT* 10 (2): 50-5, 85-6.

Lichtheim, M.
   1976 *Ancient Egyptian Literature: A Book of Readings II, The New Kingdom.* Los Angeles: University of California Press.
   1980 *Ancient Egyptian Literature: A Book of Readings III, The Late Period.* Los Angeles: University of California Press.

Manniche, L.
   1995 'Divine Reflections of Female Behaviour', *KMT* 5 (4): 52-9.

Meskell, L.
   1998 *Archaeologies of Social Life: Age, Sex Class, et*

Moore, H. L.
- *cetera in Ancient Egypt*. Oxford, Blackwell Publishers.
- 1988 *Feminism and anthropology*. Cambridge: Polity Press.

Müller, C.
- 1980 'Jugendlocke', *LÄ* III: 273-4.

Nur el Din, A. H.
- 1996 *The Role of Women in the Ancient Egyptian Society*. Cairo, SCA Press.

Pinch, G.
- 1993 *Votive Offerings to Hathor*. Oxford: Griffith institute.

Plutarch
- 1970 *De Iside et Osiride*. Translated, and with a commentary by J. G. Griffths. Cardiff: Loeb Classical Library.

Robins, G.
- 1993 *Women in Ancient Egypt*. London: British Museum Press.
- 1995 'Women & Children in Peril: Pregnancy, Birth & Infant Mortality in Ancient Egypt', *KMT* 5 (4): 29-39.
- 1996 'Dress, Undress, and the Representation of Fertility and Potency in New Kingdom Art,' in N. B. Kampen (ed.). *Sexuality in Ancient Art*. Cambridge: Cambridge University Press: 29-39.
- 1997 *The Art of Ancient Egypt*. London: British Museum Press.

Roth, A. M.
- 1991 *Egyptian Phyles in the Old Kingdom: The Evolution of a System of Social Organization*. Chicago: Oriental Institute of the University of Chicago Press.
- 1992 'The *psš-kf* and the 'Opening of the Mouth' Ceremony: a ritual of birth and rebirth,' *JEA* 78: 113-47.

Schäfer, H.
- 1986 *Principles of Egyptian Art*. Oxford: Oxford University Press.

Schiegel, A. & Barry, H, III,
- 1979 'Adolescent Initiation Ceremonies: A Cross-Cultural Code', *Ethnology* 18: 199-210.

Sethe, K. & Helck, W.
- 1906-58 *Urkunden der ägyptischen Alterums IV: Urkunden der 18. Dynastie*. Leipzig & Berlin: Verlag Engelmann.

Slater, P. E.
- 1992 *The Glory of Hera, Greek Mythology and the Greek Family*. Princeton: Princeton University Press.

Smith, W. S.
- 1980 *The Art and Architecture of Ancient Egypt*. (Revised by W. K. Simpson). London: Yale University Press.

Springborg, P.
- 1990 *Royal Persons: Patriarchal Monarchy and the Feminine Principle*. London: Unwin Hyman.

Strouhal, E.
- 1992 *Life in Ancient Egypt*. London: Opus Publishing Ltd.

Tower Hollis, S.
- 1995 'Five goddesses in the Third Millennium B.C.', *KMT* 5 (4): 46-51, 82-5.

Trigger, B. G.
- 1993 *Early Civilizations: Ancient Egypt in Context*. Cairo: American University in Cairo Press.

Vandier, J.
- 1958 *Manual d'archéologie égyptienne III: Les grandes époques. La statuarie*. Paris: A. & J. Picard.

Wilkinson, T. A. H.
- 1999 *Early Dynastic Egypt*. London: Routledge.

MORPHOLOGICAL VARIATION IN EGYPTIAN CRANIA

Sonia Zakrzewski

Introduction

Cranial morphology has been used to assess the genetic composition and affinity of populations where actual DNA evidence is unavailable. Usually these studies have been geographically cross-sectional, allowing similarities between populations to be assessed.[1] This study has attempted to assess population changes through time, to understand how Egyptian populations relate to each other through time. This paper will therefore question whether the metric morphological evidence suggests that there is direct population continuity through the transition from the Predynastic periods through to the Dynastic periods.

Many previous studies of Egyptian crania have been undertaken.[2] Most of the early studies either employed simple estimates of shape conforming to pre-imposed "types", such as Semitic or Hamitic.[3] Later studies employed metric characters, but used the now discredited Coefficient of Racial Likeness.[4] Most of these early studies tried to estimate whether ancient Egyptian crania were more similar to Europeans or tropical Africans. More recent studies have either used particular samples of Egyptians as out-groups in order to ask similar questions,[5] or have attempted to compare Egyptians with other groups using the actual metric measurements of individuals, rather than group means.[6] Unsurprisingly, morphological similarities have been found between Upper Egyptians and Nubians,[7] and between Egyptians and southern Africans.[8]

This study however has attempted to understand population change through time within the Nile Valley. Thus the a priori assumption is that morphological similarities will be found between successive populations, indicating population continuity in Upper Egypt over the time period concerned.

Materials and Methods

Due to difficulties in obtaining accurate dates for many of the skeletons available for study in university and museum collection, only rough dates have been employed in the present study. The time periods are thus broken down into Badari, Early Predynastic (EPD), Late Predynastic (LPD), Archaic Period, Old Kingdom (OK), Middle Kingdom (MK) and Twenty-sixth to Thirtieth Dynasties (Late). The sample sizes are shown in Table 1.

Period	N	Samples	Collections[9]	Source
Badari	49	El-Badari	Duckworth	SRZ
EPD	80	Abydos, El-Amrah & Gebelein	NHM & Marro	SRZ
LPD	72	Abydos, El-Amrah & Hierakonpolis	NHM & Duckworth	SRZ
Archaic	97	Abydos	NHM & Duckworth	SRZ
OK	85	Regagnah, Meidum & Gizeh	NHM & Reisner	SRZ
MK	22	Gebelein	Marro	SRZ
Late	111	Gizeh	Duckworth	Howells[10]

Table 1. Sample Sizes for the Populations Studied

Only adults were measured, with maturity being assessed either by fusion of the sphenooccipital synchondrosis or by full eruption of the third molars. All individuals were assigned a sex. Where possible this was undertaken through inspection of associated pelvic material, but were this was lacking, individuals were graded on the basis of cranial features such as the development of the supraorbital and glabellar region, the squareness of the anterior portion of the mandible, flaring of the gonial region and the robusticity of the nuchal region. Where cranial selection was possible due to reasonable sample sizes, crania were selected in order of completeness.

The measurements taken were all either metric measurements of size,[11] or grades of cranial robusticity.[12] Non-metric traits were not assessed as these have been shown to be less reliable in assessing population affinity than metric measurements[13]. In total up to 71 measurements were taken of cranial size and shape, including cranial height and breadth, facial height, breadth and protrusion and basicranial dimensions. 8 measures of cranial robusticity were collected, on a graded scale, and 11 mandibular measurements were taken including lengths and thickness.[14]

---

[1] E.g. Howells 1973, 1989, 1995; Lahr 1996; Warusawithana-Kulatilake 2000.
[2] For further details see chapter 5 of Zakrzewski 2001.
[3] E.g. Randall-MacIver 1901; Thomson and Randall-MacIver 1905.
[4] E.g. Batrawi 1945, 1946; Morant 1925, 1935, 1937, 63-66.
[5] Howells 1973, 1989.
[6] Hillson 1978; Keita 1990, 1992.
[7] Billy 1977; Hillson 1978.
[8] Hillson 1978; Keita 1990, 1992.

[9] Where Duckworth refers to the collections of the Dept of Biological Anthropology, Cambridge University, NHM to the collections of the Natural History Museum, London, Marro to the Marro collection of the Dept of Anthropology, Turin, Italy, and, Reisner to the Reisner collections of the Naturhistorisches Museum in Vienna, Austria.
[10] Data kindly provided by W.W. Howells from his global database of cranial metric measurements.
[11] Following Howells 1973, 1989.
[12] Following Lahr 1996.
[13] Powell 1989; Rightmire 1976.
[14] For full listing of measurements see Zakrzewski 2001, 87-9. For full description see Howells 1973, 170-87 & Lahr 1996, 341-52.

Sonia Zakrzewski

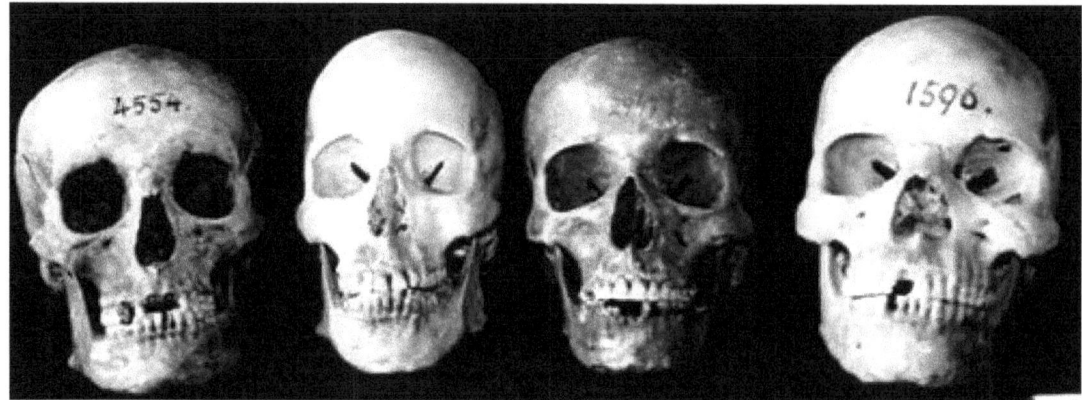

Figure 1. Global Cranial Variation.
(Specimens VL4554 from Germany, 99/6962 from India, VL2947 from El-Hesa, Egypt & VL1596 from German East Africa, all in the American Museum of Natural History, NY. Courtesy of I. Ribot).

Figure 1 (at rear) indicates the type of morphological variation found between a randomly selected sample of crania. The morphological differences between the populations can clearly be seen, especially the differences in terms of cranial and facial breadth.

Results

Both univariate and multivariate analyses were undertaken. Univariate analyses were undertaken initially to get some impression of the patterning of morphological change through time. Cranial indices correct to some extent for absolute size differences, and therefore allow changes in shape to be recognised. Most of the traditional cranial indices showed significant differences through time. Figure 2 indicates the pattern in change of the cranial index (CRI) through time.[15] This figure indicates that through time the crania increase in breadth relative to cranial length ($N = 488$, $p<0.001$), thus making the crania appear more globular through time. A similar pattern has been found in Nubian material over a larger time period, from the Mesolithic to Christian periods.[16]

Univariate analysis of variance was undertaken on all metric variables. Two variables were discarded as the only significant differences through time were found between the Late material and all the earlier group. Discrepancies in measuring technique could therefore not be excluded from possible causality of this significance, and thus the variables had to be excluded from analysis. Of the remaining 69 variables, only six did not exhibit statistically significant change through the time periods considered. An example of this change is shown in Figure 3, below. For most of the variables the Archaic periods and Late periods exhibit notably different morphologies than the neighbouring time groups.

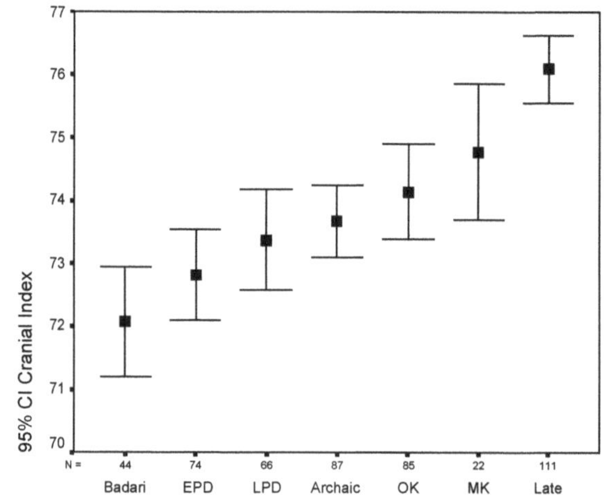

Figure 2. CRI, with sexes pooled, with 95% confidence intervals.

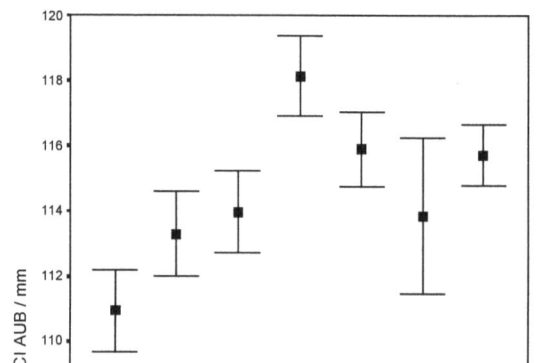

Figure 3. Change through time in biauricular breadth (AUB), sexes pooled, with 95% confidence intervals.

---

[15] Where $CRI = \dfrac{100 * XCB}{GOL}$, when XCB refer to maximum cranial breadth, and GOL to glabello-occipital length.

[16] Carlson 1976, 475-82; Carlson and Van-Gerven 1977, 501-4.

The multivariate analyses undertaken are principal components analysis (PCA) and discriminant function analysis (DFA). The former acts by considering groups of variables and tries to explain the variance seen in those variables. PCA is a form of factor analysis that aims to identify the underlying factors (variables) explaining the pattern of correlations within the set of observed variables. It can therefore be employed to ascertain which variables are of greatest importance in explaining the variance seen within the ellipse of data points in multidimensional space. PCA has therefore been employed to screen the variables employed to understand how great a contribution each variable makes to the variance in morphology.

By contrast, the purpose of DFA is to assign group membership from a number of predictors, thus here it has been used to assess whether cranial variables can be used to predict the time period group membership of the cranial sample. The main aim is to find the dimension or dimensions by which the groups differ and then derive classification functions from this to predict group membership. DFA forms a string of functions and judges whether the groups it predicts from these functions match the imposed groups within the data. Thus, in DFA, the raw measurements for each individual are converted into functions relating to cranial dimensions. A coefficient (weighting) is given to each measurement (variable) and the individual's actual measurement is multiplied by this coefficient. The sum of these weighted measurements comprises the individual's 'discriminant score'. The number of discriminant functions obtained is always one fewer than the number of groups imposed on the data (in the present study, usually seven time periods and hence six functions)Pooled sex analyses were initially undertaken on the complete data set, employing all suitable variables in order to ascertain how different the time period groups actually were. A PCA of all the major fifty two metric variables derived twelve components with Eigenvalues > 1. These were able to account for 76.3% of the variance found within the cranial samples. Of greatest importance are the variables that code for cranial length and breadth, and facial prognathism. This analysis indicated that the earlier populations, such as the Badari and EPD, generally had shorter cranial lengths than the later samples. The Archaic period samples have the greatest expression of midfacial prognathism. The Late group crania have greater cranial breadth than the other samples. DFA was undertaken employing the same variables. The first two functions derived are plotted in Figure 4. These two functions account for 50.8% and 20.5% of the variance respectively. Overall the six functions derived were able to correctly classify 87.5% of the crania into their time period group. This suggests that actual morphological differences exist between the various groups. The classification table is shown in Table 2 (at rear).

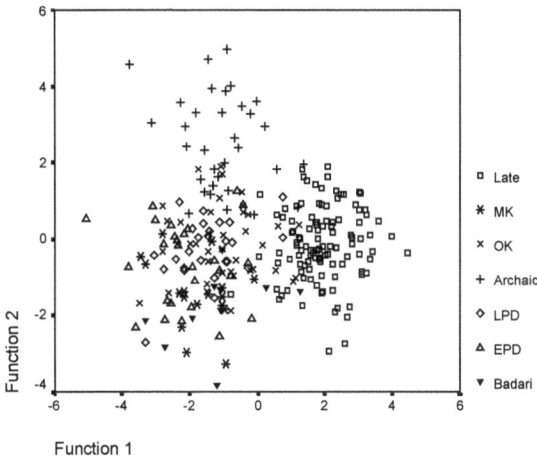

Figure 4. Plot of the first two functions derived by DFA, pooled sexes.

The next series of analyses concentrated over the period of State formation, and so only included samples from the Badari through to the Archaic periods. In order to maximise the amount of available information given the fragmentary nature of some of these crania, oneway analysis of variance was initially undertaken to assess which variables exhibited statistically significant differences between these periods. PCA and DFA were then undertaken only employing these variables.

PCA derived nine components, which together were able to account for 75.6% of the variance within the cranial morphology of the individuals ($N = 98$). The first two components are plotted in Figure 5, below, with ellipses drawn around the Badari and Archaic clusters. The first component accounts for 37.7% of the variance, and codes mainly for cranial length and facial breadth. It is also affected by facial prognathism, and codes for the midfacial form. The second component only accounts for 8.7% of the variance, and codes mainly for cranial

Original Group	Predicted Group Membership						
	Badari	EPD	LPD	Archaic	OK	MK	Late
Badari	90.0	.0	0.0	.0	.0	.0	10.0
EPD	.0	81.5	7.4	7.4	.0	3.7	.0
LPD	.0	7.7	80.8	.0	7.7	3.8	.0
Archaic	.0	3.0	.0	87.9	.0	.0	9.1
OK	.0	7.7	7.7	5.1	64.1	5.1	10.3
MK	.0	11.8	.0	.0	.0	88.2	.0
Late	.0	.9	.0	.0	.9	.0	98.2

Table 2. Percentage of crania correctly classified by DFA of all time period groups, sexes pooled.

breadth and facial flatness (i.e. highly prognathic individuals lie low on PC 2). Figure 5 therefore shows that distinct morphological differences exist between the various groups, with the Archaic group having the largest crania, especially in terms of length and facial breadth. DFA derived three functions that together were able to correctly classify 93.9% of the crania into their time period group on the basis of their morphologies.

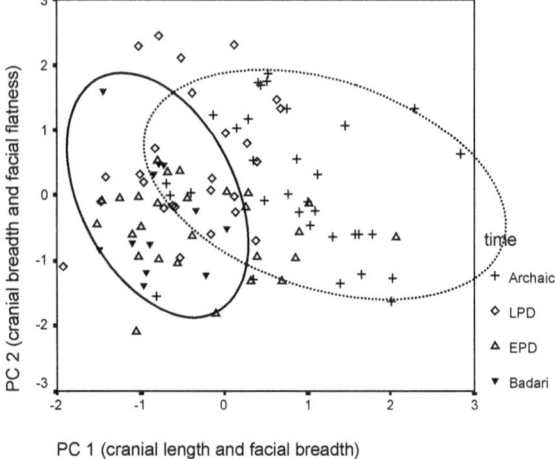

Figure 5. Plot of first two components for Badari to Archaic periods, sexes pooled.

Analyses were then undertaken adding in the OK sample. Again oneway analysis of variance was undertaken to ascertain which variables were responsible for the morphological differences between the time periods, and hence to maximise the resolution of discrimination. The PCA was able to account for 73.9% of the variance seen with nine components (with Eigenvalues > 1). DFA, employing the same set of variables, using four functions, was able to correctly classify 87.5% of the crania into their original time period group. The first two functions, accounting cumulatively for 72.4% of the variance, are plotted in Figure 6. This figure shows that, apart from one outlier, the Badari form a distinct population cluster. The EPD group mainly exhibits morphological similarity with the LPD population. Greater morphological overlap is seen between the LPD, Archaic and OK samples.

Discussion

The cranial evidence described above indicates that distinct morphological patterns are seen within time-successive Nile Valley populations. This paper has concentrated on the period of state formation as the processes involved have been much debated. The prevailing views have changed through time, from complete population replacement by an invasion of a Dynastic race,[17] to local indigenous development, particularly of the Upper Egyptian region expanding northwards.[18]

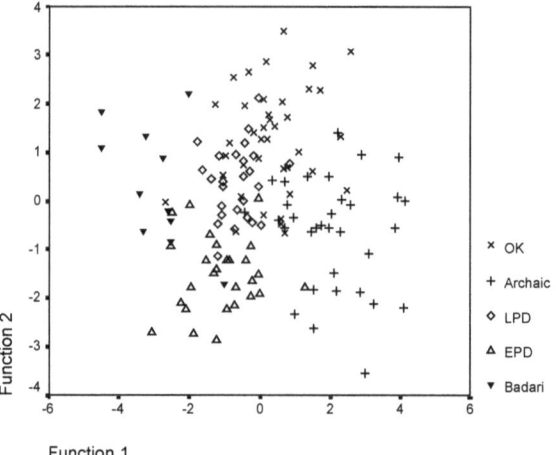

Figure 6. Plot of the first two functions for Badari to OK periods, sexes pooled.

The morphological overlapping between populations in the analyses described above indicates that some population continuity existed through the time periods considered. Certain distinct morphological differences also exists between the various samples, indicating that some evidence for changes in the genetic composition of the Nile valley population are likely. Through time, however, certain trends could be seen within the samples implying that there was not a wave of migration into the area with population replacement, but rather that there was gradual population assimilation with other groups.

Non-metric traits have been considered as reasonable proxies for genetics when genetic data is unavailable.[19] Greater similarity has been found between Dynastic samples at Assyut and Gebelein than between either Dynastic group and a Predynastic sample from Gebelein,[20] suggesting some degree of genetic change through time. This work supports the distinction of the Archaic group from the preceding Predynastic samples described in this paper. Genetic continuity has been described between Badari, Naqada and Hierakonpolis samples, and between Archaic and OK populations, but with genetic discontinuity from the New Kingdom onwards.[21] This study of epigenetic traits supports the genetic separation of the Late group from the early cranial samples, as shown in Figure 4.

Studies of classical genetic markers, such as ABO blood groups, within modern populations have shown that modern Egyptians form a sister group to a variety of populations including Nubians, Moroccans, Libyans and

---

[17] Derry 1956, 81; Petrie 1900, 1901, 1939; Winkler 1938, 1939.

[18] Kemp 1989; Wilkinson 1996, 95.
[19] Some studies have shown that these traits are less reliable than the metric method employed in this paper (e.g. Powell 1989; Rightmire 1976).
[20] Reggio, Masali and Chiarelli 1969, 200-202.
[21] Berry and Berry 1972, 203.

Canary Islanders.[22] This study shows that modern Egyptians exhibit population affinities with all North African groups, and should thus be considered in relation to other such populations. Evidence from non-coding sections of mitochondrial DNA (mtDNA) from modern Nile Valley groups shows clinal change from north to south, providing evidence of population movements both up and down the valley, and suggesting either greater or more recent migrations from south to north.[23] Archaeological mtDNA has been extracted that also suggests south to north migration along the river valley.[24]

Conclusions

Distinct morphological differences occur within Egyptian populations, and hence direct and full genetic continuity throughout Egyptian history and prehistory cannot be assumed. Two distinct periods of morphological change have been found. The first corresponds to the period of state formation, as the Archaic sample has been shown to be morphological distinct from the earlier Predynastic groups. This apparent morphological separation between these periods suggests that some new individuals may have interbred with the indigenous population, thereby increasing the Egyptian gene pool. The second period of morphological disjunction occurs between the MK and the Late period, and thus can easily be related to population migrations into Egypt.

This paper has further shown that cranial morphology can be employed to further understanding of population affinity and population changes within the context of a series of time-successive populations. Even simply studying pooled sex groupings, rather than analysing each sex independently, the differences between the time periods groups are large enough that analyses can be undertaken that correctly predict their group membership.

The research undertaken has shown that biological and anthropological methods can be applied to aid in answering Egyptological questions. Egypt has environmental conditions that permit reasonable preservation of skeletal material and thus permit relatively clear and complete data to be collected. In the past, this material has been rarely studied in the context of Egyptology, but rather has been analysed in terms of evolutionary problems. Egyptian archaeology, with its wealth of literary and pictorial evidence, has rarely relied, or even considered, the scientific evidence for the day-to-day lives of the original populations. In the future it is hoped to further integrate biological methodologies into research topics such as recognition of social ranking differences and self-perception in artistic representation.

Acknowledgements

The author would like to thank Drs R Foley and M Lahr (Dept of Biological Anthropology) for their discussions and help. Sincere thanks are given to all those who permitted the study of the collections in their care; Mrs M Bellatti (Duckworth Laboratory, Cambridge), Dr L Humphrey & Mr R Kruszynski (NHM, London), Dr E Rabino-Massa & Ms R Boano (Marro Collection, Turin) & Dr M Teschler-Nicola (Reisner Collection, Vienna). A Bioarchaeology Award from the Wellcome Trust funded this research.

Sonia Zakrzewski
University of Durham

Cited Works

Batrawi, A.
   1945 'The Racial History of Egypt and Nubia', *Journal of the Royal Anthropological Institute of Great Britain and Ireland* 75:81-101.
   1946 'The Racial History of Egypt and Nubia: Part II. The Racial Relationships of the Ancient and Modern Populations of Egypt and Nubia',*Journal of the Royal Anthropological Institute of Great Britain and Ireland* 76:131-156.

Berry A.C. and R. J. Berry.
   1972 'Origins and Relationships of the Ancient Egyptians. Based on a Study of Non-metrical Variations in the Skull', *Journal of Human Evolution* 1:199-208.

Billy, G.
   1977 'Population Changes in Egypt and Nubia', *Journal of Human Evolution* 6:697-704.

Carlson, D.S.
   1976 'Temporal Variation in Prehistoric Nubian Crania', *American Journal of Physical Anthropology* 45:467-484.

Carlson, D.S. and D. P. van-Gerven.
   1977 'Masticatory Function and Post-Pleistocene Evolution in Nubia', *American Journal of Physical Anthropology* 46:495-506.

Cavalli-Sforza, L.L., A. Piazza, and P. Menozzi.
   1994 *The History and Geography of Human Genes.* Princeton: Princeton University Press.

Derry, D.E.
   1956 'The Dynastic Race in Egypt', *JEA* 42:80-85.

Fox, C.L.
   1997 'mtDNA Analysis in Ancient Nubians Supports the Existence of Gene Flow Between Sub-Sahara and North Africa in the Nile Valley', *Annals of Human Biology* 24:217-227.

Hillson, S.W.
   1978 *Human Biological Variation in the Nile Valley, in Relation to Environmental Factors.* PhD Thesis, London University, London.

---

[22] Cavalli-Sforza, Menozzi and Piazza 1994, 169-174.
[23] Krings et al 1999, 1172-1175.
[24] Fox 1997, 224.

Howells, W.W.
- 1973 *Cranial Variation in Man: A Study by Multivariate Analysis of Patterns of Difference Among Recent Human Populations.* Papers of the Peabody Museum of Archaeology and Ethnology, Harvard University 67.
- 1989 *Skull Shapes and the Map: Craniometric Analyses in the Dispersion of Modern Homo.* Peabody Museum Papers, Harvard University 79.
- 1995 *Who's Who in Skulls: Ethnic Identification of Crania from Measurements.* Papers of the Peabody Museum of Archaeology and Ethnology, Harvard University 82.

Keita, S.O.Y.
- 1990 'Studies of Ancient Crania from Northern Africa', *American Journal of Physical Anthropology* 83:35-48.
- 1992 'Further Studies of Crania From Ancient Northern Africa: An Analysis of Crania From First Dynasty Egyptian Tombs, Using Multiple Discriminant Functions', *American Journal of Physical Anthropology* 87:245-254.

Kemp, B.J.
- 1989 *Ancient Egypt: Anatomy of a Civilization.* London: Routledge.

Krings, M. et al.
- 1999 'mtDNA Analysis of Nile River Valley Populations: A Genetic Corridor or a Barrier to Migration?' *American Journal of Human Genetics* 64:1166-1176.

Lahr, M.M.
- 1996 *The Evolution of Modern Human Diversity.* Cambridge: Cambridge University Press.

Morant, G.M.
- 1925 'A Study of Egyptian Craniology from Prehistoric to Roman Times', *Biometrika* 17:1-52.
- 1935 'A Study of Predynastic Egyptian Skulls from Badari Based on Measurements Taken by Miss B. N. Stoessiger and Professor D. E. Derry', *Biometrika* 27:293-309.
- 1937 The Predynastic Egyptian Skulls from Badari and Their Racial Affinities. In G Brunton (ed.): Mostagedda and the Tasian Culture. London: Quaritch.

Petrie, W.M.F.
- 1900 *The Royal Tombs of the First Dynasty.* London: Egypt Exploration Fund.
- 1901 *The Royal Tombs of the Earliest Dynasties.* London: Egypt Exploration Fund.
- 1939 *The Making of Egypt.* London: Sheldon Press.

Powell, J.E.
- 1989 *Metric Versus Non-Metric Skeletal Traits: Which is the More Reliable Indicator of Genetic Distance? With Special Reference to Crania from Ancient Greece and Egypt.* Unpublished Ph.D. thesis, Bristol University.

Randall-MacIver, D.
- 1901 *The Earliest Inhabitants of Abydos: A Craniological Study.* Oxford: Clarendon Press.

Reggio G, M. Masali, and B. Chiarelli.
- 1969 'Caratteri Epigenetici del Cranio Degli Antichi Egizi e Loro Interesse Etnico' *Rivista di Antropologia* 56:199-202.

Rightmire, G.P.
- 1976 'Metric versus Discrete Traits in African Skulls', in Giles, E. and J.S. Friedlaender (eds.), *The Measures of Man.* Cambridge MA: Peabody Museum Press.

Thomson, A. and D. Randall-MacIver
- 1905 *The Ancient Races of the Thebaid: Being an Anthropometrical Study of the Inhabitants of Upper Egypt.* Oxford: Clarendon Press.

Warusawithana-Kulatilake, S.D.
- 2000 *Cranial Diversity and the Evolutionary History of South Asians.* Ph.D. thesis, Cambridge University.

Wilkinson, T.A.H.
- 1996 *State Formation in Egypt: Chronology and Society.* BAR International Series 651. Oxford: BAR Publishing.

Winkler, H.A.
- 1938 *Rock-Drawings of Southern Upper Egypt.* London: Oxford University Press.
- 1939 *Rock-Drawings of Southern Upper Egypt.* London: Oxford University Press.

Zakrzewski, S.R.
- 2001 *Continuity and Change: A Biological History of Ancient Egypt.* Unpublished Ph.D. thesis, Cambridge University.